AF251237

OUTLINES OF RUSSIAN CULTURE
Volume III

The Origins of Ideology

By Paul Miliukov

Edited & Translated by

JOSEPH L. WIECZYNSKI

With

The Two Worlds of Paul Miliukov

By

JOSEPH T. FUHRMANN

Academic International Press

1974

THE RUSSIAN SERIES / Volume 19

Paul N. Miliukov **OUTLINES OF RUSSIAN CULTURE
THE ORIGINS OF IDEOLOGY** Translation of *Ocherki
russkoi kulturi* (Paris, 1930-1937), Volume 3, pp. 1-155

Library of Congress Catalog Card Number: 74-81632
ISBN: O-87569-056-4

Printed in the United States of America

ACADEMIC INTERNATIONAL PRESS
Box 555 Gulf Breeze Florida 32561

FOR JO WIECZYNSKI

CONTENTS

CONTENTS

THE TWO WORLDS OF PAUL MILIUKOV

Nietzsche said that "the professor in politics always plays
the comic role." Had he extended his thoughts to historians
the German sage might have added to this the observation
that historians as politicians seldom make history successfully.
Paul Miliukov could be taken as a case in point, a man who
lived simultaneously in the world of the historian and the
world of the statesman. One of the greatest and most original
Russian historians, Miliukov might be said to have failed as
a politician. Of course, this "failure" — if failure it was — was
that of an entire generation and no more the sole product of
Miliukov's frailties than of his strengths. Miliukov was not
a mere closet scholar engaging, as Russell Kirk has said of some
learned souls, in "the presumption of giving commands to
armies and decrees to nations." Nor was he what Kirk would
call "a pure-bred metaphysician, devoid of reverence and
humility." We must search further in these two worlds to find
Miliukov's true measure.

Paul Miliukov sifted state power in his hands. His political career began as the leader of Russian liberalism as represented by the Constitutional Democratic (Kadet) Party.
Elected three times to Russia's legislative Duma, finally in
1917 he became minister of foreign affairs in the Provisional
Government. Throughout his stormy career Miliukov was
humble in the face of what he saw to be his country's fundamental problem, that of harnessing constitutionalism to a
society undergoing explosive modernization. By 1916 Miliukov knew that Russia had plunged into a profound crisis.
But Russia was no stranger to crises, and when they had

occurred in the past the people rallied, invaders were repelled, and from it all emerged a new order not so dissimilar to the old. Miliukov the historian knew all this quite well. But did his understanding of the Russian past serve Miliukov the states-man as a reliable guide to the nation's present and future? Or did it serve him too well?

Paul Nikolaevich Miliukov was born in Moscow into the fam-ily of an architect on January 15, 1859. He attended Moscow University from 1877 to 1882. One of the few professors who exercised some professional influence on Miliukov was Paul Vinogradov, the eminent student of medieval English agricul-ture who left Russia in 1902, became Corpus professor of jurisprudence at Oxford in 1903 and died in Paris in 1925. Vi-nogradov offered Paul Nikolaevich friendship and support and probably encouraged Miliukov's life-long tendency to draw con-trasts between medieval England and Russia, the point of which was always to emphasize how different was the history of the two countries. During his first year at Moscow University, Mil-iukov fell under the spell of the lectures of Sergei Soloviev, then finishing the twenty-ninth and final volume of his master-ful *History of Russia from the Earliest Times.* Soloviev did not lead Miliukov to become a member of the "state school" of Russian historians, of which Soloviev was the most eminent representative. But Soloviev may have helped to persuade the younger man that in Russia the state had played a far more commanding role than was the case in Western Europe.

Miliukov's relations with Vasily Kliuchevsky, the domi-nant intellectual figure of the history faculty while Miliukov was a student at Moscow University, were extremely complex. Their personal relations began well but steadily deteriorated, which gives little cause for surprise considering the differences between the two men. Kliuchevsky was neither a liberal nor a cosmopolite, nor was he receptive, as was Miliukov, to the charms of such "moderns" as Karl Marx or Auguste Comte. Moreover, although Kliuchevsky maintained a purely objective attitude when writing on the subject, he did not share Miliukov's personal sympathy for the "westernization" of Russia at the time of Peter the Great. (In a reversal of what might be expected of their roles, however, the skeptical Miliukov was far more sensitive than Kliuchevsky to the role of religion and the church in early Russia; Kliuchevsky's work often ignores religious developments whereas Miliukov treats them in great detail).

The discord between Kliuchevsky and Miliukov reached a high point in 1892 when Miliukov presented as his doctoral dissertation *The National Economy of Russia during the First Quarter of the Eighteenth Century and the Reforms of Peter the Great.* Based on exhaustive archival research, this vast study shed considerable light on the entire scope of the Petrine reforms, and in published form it drew immediate recognition as a landmark of historical literature. For reasons which remain unclear, Kliuchevsky insisted that Miliukov be awarded only the master's degree for this work, and that he prepare another dissertation for the doctorate. Miliukov's friend and admirer, Sergei Platonov of the University of St. Petersburg, persuaded the faculty of this university to bestow the higher degree on Miliukov for his *National Economy,* which as a book won a large cash prize. The obstacles which Kliuchevsky threw in his path affected Miliukov's entire career. "Something seems to have snapped in Miliukov's eagerness for the professor's calling," says Miliukov's biographer, Thomas Riha, of the 1892 experience, and when Miliukov "abandoned it for politics, the pain was minimal." Miliukov always esteemed Kliuchevsky highly as an historian and they eventually resumed their friendship, but on a different basis than in earlier years.

By this time, in fact, Miliukov doubted that the historical profession could satisfy fully his interests and ambitions. Kliuchevsky probably continued to stimulate Miliukov's desire for recognition as a publishing historian. Still, the younger man was coming to see the study of history not as an end in itself, but as a political instrument to be used to shape Russia's future. The decade of the 1890s was an exciting time at Moscow University

and, while teaching there, Miliukov plunged into the liberal
movement then struggling to reform the government of
Alexander III and Nicholas II. This involvement brought
about a decisive turn in Miliukov's career: as punishment for
his political activities Miliukov was dismissed from the faculty in 1895. During the next decade he lectured at foreign
universities (including Chicago and Harvard) and contributed
to Russian liberal publications issued in Western Europe.
More than any other Russian of his day Miliukov represented
to liberal intellectuals of the West the political aspirations
of "progressive" Russia.

The Revolution of 1905 found Miliukov in Chicago.
Losing not a moment, he hurried to Russia to play a stellar
role there in the struggle for reform. In succeeding years
Miliukov was elected to the first Duma, the Russian legislative
assembly granted by the tsar in October 1905 as a concession
to the revolutionaries, and to the third and fourth Dumas as
well. Miliukov was the most prominent leader of Russia's new
liberal party, the Constitutional Democrats, known as "Kadets"
from the abbreviation of their party name. After 1907 Miliukov edited the Kadet journal *Rech'* (Speech), and in these
years it seemed to many that in time Miliukov would become
chief minister of Russia. When the war broke out in 1914,
Miliukov withdrew his opposition to Nicholas' government
and pledged, as he says in his *Memoirs*, unconditional support
"for the liberation of our fatherland from foreign invasion,
for the liberation of Europe and the Slavs from German domination, for the liberation of the whole world from the in-
tolerable strain of ever-growing armament." As Russian defeats
mounted, however, Miliukov saw the need for a new government which would command broad public support and thus be
able to mobilize the nation's resources and win the war. At
an excited meeting of the Duma on November 1, 1916, Miliukov delivered one of the most important speeches in Russian
history: cataloging unbelievable setbacks and mistakes of
recent months, at each point he shouted the inflamatory

question "Is this stupidity or is this treason?" This devastating speech weakened the Romanov regime still further, for it served to signal the shift of the moderates into renewed opposition.

The tsar's government fell in February 1917. A "Provisional Government" was then created, headed by a cabinet of prominent statesmen who proposed to administer the most pressing affairs of state until a constituent assembly could be called to draft a permanent constitution and government for Russia. In those turbulent days Miliukov lived fully in the world of the statesman, for he was appointed minister of foreign affairs. His policy in this office was to renew active Russian participation in the war against Germany, so that when peace came Russia would receive the concessions promised her at the beginning of the war, especially the Dardanelles, which would give access from the Black Sea to the Mediterranean. The revolutionary idealism sweeping Russia in 1917 collided with "imperialist" war aims such as these. The new foreign minister received the sarcastic nickname "Miliukov of the Dardanelles," and after only two months in power he was forced to resign.

Miliukov was appalled by the Bolshevik seizure of power in October 1917, seeing in it an undemocratic act which would destroy the nation's finest cultural and political traditions. He fled south to join the battle of the "white" generals against the "reds," and at a late point in the civil war even tried to enlist German military aid against the communists. Miliukov departed Russia in 1920, finally settling in Paris where again he energetically took to the pen and lecture circuit to interpret Russia's woes, past and present, to western liberals. For the next two decades Miliukov insisted that "the struggle against Bolshevism must continue until the liberation of Russia." When Hitler attacked his homeland in 1941, however, Miliukov fervently called for the victory of the U.S.S.R. The Soviet historian, N. F. Slavin, with a touch of pride, I think, notes that in an article written not

long before his death in occupied France on March 31, 1943,
Paul Nikolaevich Miliukov "recognized the successes of the
Soviet government and the Red Army.

Miliukov was too much of an individualist to identify himself
with any single "school" of Russian historians, and political
distractions prevented him from leaving a "school" of his own.
But he was a prolific writer, and even the briefest bibliography
of his contributions suggests the broad nature of his interests.
Miliukov brought together the world of the scholar and the
world of the political activist in such works as *Russia and its
Crisis* (1905) and *Russia Today and Tomorrow* (1922), books
which used the past to explicate the present and predict the
future. His wide-ranging intellectual interests led him to write
The Living Pushkin (1937), several studies of the Russian intelligentsia, and a major historiographical work (*Main Tendencies of Russian Historical Thought*, 1897). In these studies
the writing of history in Russia is portrayed as an integral part
of Russian intellectual history. Among Miliukov's most important efforts is his three-volume *History of Russia* (English
translation, 1968-1969), parts of which were written by colleagues. The stated purpose of this work is that of acquaint-
ing western readers more thoroughly with the Russian past,
a mission to which he could rightly claim to have devoted
some of his best earlier labors. With this multi-volume account, contrived in the autumn of an eminent scholar's life,
Miliukov invited a comparison of his achievement with that
of the greatest Russian historians. Karamzin, Soloviev and
Kliuchevsky, and such talented contemporaries as Pokrovsky
and Rozhkov, each produced (Kliuchevsky on the basis of
lecture notes which others brought to publication) a multi-
volume history of Russia treating the major historical problems of Russia's entire past. No other work from Miliukov's
pen demonstrates more clearly his lifelong search for accomplishment and stature as an historian.
     Several of Paul Miliukov's books significantly affected

the writing of Russian history. His *National Economy of Russia* (cited above) and *Controversial Questions on the Fiscal History of the Muscovite State* (1892) were careful, factual studies based upon archival material which hitherto had not been consistently utilized. These contributions helped to shift the debate about the meaning of the Petrine reforms away from the traditional abstract moral plane (was Peter "progressive"?) to the more specific level of investigating what actually *happened* in Russia under Peter the Great. For example, Michael Bogoslovsky's important dissertation, *The Oblast Reform of Peter the Great: The Provinces from 1719 to 1727* (1902), followed Miliukov's approach in studying this period. Nonetheless, Miliukov's ultimate contribution to the understanding of Russia's past is his celebrated *Outlines of Russian Culture*, first published in three parts in St. Petersburg between 1895 and 1903, republished in Russia in several editions thereafter, then finally revised and issued in Paris in a jubilee edition between 1930 and 1937.

Because these *Outlines* for so long have played an extraordinary part in the education of cultivated Russians, it is easy to forget the relative originality of the work when it first burst upon the scholarly scene. Admittedly, the concept and methodology behind *Outlines of Russian Culture* drew on the historical vision of Auguste Comte and the organization of François Guizot's *Histoire de la civilisation en France*. Still, in terms of how Russian culture had been discussed by previous historians, Miliukov's effort represented a dramatic departure, for he labored to relate in a novel way (through suggestion rather than explicit statement) the past and present *and* to synthesize in a whole vision the composite elements of the nation's culture — literature, painting, architecture, music, religion and the church, social consciousness and national ideology. This was an ambitious undertaking; yet the degree of success with which Miliukov discusses all these problems is striking. In 1942 an abridged English translation of the first two parts of the *Outlines* covering the arts, literature and religion, was published in the United States. But to quote Thomas Riha, a prominent authority on Miliukov, the "third volume is his masterpiece." The translation of that volume, first begun here under the appropriate title *Outlines of Russian Culture: The Origins of Ideology*, fills a broad gap in the offerings of the greatest Russian historians available in English.

In the present volume Miliukov accords particular attention to the relationship between ideology and the rise of the Muscovite state. From the most obscure origins the principality of Moscow had bought and bullied its way by 1300 to the political forefront in northern Russia. In the next two centuries the princes of Moscow brought to successful conclusion two closely interrelated developments: "gathering the Russian lands" (subjugation of neighboring principalities) and terminating Russia's subordination to the Mongols. In this process Moscow laid claim to the legacy of the "Mother of Russian Towns," Kiev, the southern city which from the ninth to the thirteenth century had been the center of a loose federation of Russian principalities. The ruler of Kiev had borne the title "Grand Prince" (*velikii kniaz*) as a sign of suzerainty over his "brothers," the princes of other cities and principalities who were also descendants of Rurik who, many historians agree, had founded the entire dynasty in the ninth century. Beginning with Ivan I (1325-1341), the prince of Moscow styled himself "Grand Prince of All Russia," something of a fiction, of course, if for no reason other than the fact that the western portion of the Kievan realm had come under the rule of Poland and Lithuania. Miliukov indicates the diplomatic problems generated between Poland-Lithuania and Muscovite Russia by the expansionist ambitions implicit in the title of the Russian autocrat. Not until the seventeenth century did Moscow succeed in regaining the land Kiev had lost to Lithuania and Poland four centuries before.

The Russian church played an important role in the rise of the Muscovite state. The city of Kiev had been the see of the

"Metropolitan of Kiev and All Russia," the leader of the Russian church. But even before the Mongol conquest of 1237-1242 Kiev had declined in economic and political power, and from the time of Cyril II (1242-1281) metropolitans examined the question of moving north. In 1305 Metropolitan Peter allied himself with Yury, prince of Moscow. Peter permanently relocated his "residence and choir" in Moscow, and in 1326 consented to be buried in the city. Thus did Moscow gain the prestige of becoming the new seat of the church, an important development since the church was the one institution in Russia whose material and ideological interests were wholly Russian, transcending the constantly shifting boundaries of numerous and feuding principalities. In future decades the church came more and more to support the cause of the prince of Moscow as likewise the cause of all good Russian Christians.

No less significant was the contribution of the church in developing the ideology which accompanied the rise of Moscow, an ideology which by the late 1400s represented Moscow as the "Third Rome," the sole remaining center of true Christianity. The sources of this important doctrine are complex and stem indirectly from the pretensions of Constantinople, which had been founded in the fourth century A.D. to serve as the new capital of the Roman empire. After the empire converted to Christianity the Bishop of Rome and the Patriarch of Constantinople fell into constant and serious disagreement, and by the mid-1100s into outright schism. Constantinople was by then representing itself not merely as a "new" or "second" Rome, but as the *only* Rome. In this view the original Rome had betrayed the faith, the defense of which therefore had passed to the East. After 1204 the Russian church vigorously supported Greek claims, though this was not solely due to the fact that the Russian church was under the Patriarch of Constantinople. From the time Russia was converted under Byzantine auspices in the tenth century Russians consistently pursued friendly relations with Rome; but when Christian crusaders from the West took and plundered Constantinople in 1204, the shock was such as to cause Russia to turn on the Latins and to support the religious position of the Greeks in a new and uncritical way.

During the fifteenth century calamities on a colossal scale overtook Constantinople, and these affected Russia's concept of its relationship to the two traditional centers of Christianity. In exchange for a papal promise to raise forces in the West to save Constantinople from the Turks (who were clearly about to take the city), the Greeks submitted to reunification of the church on terms dictated by the Pope at the Council of Florence in 1439. Thereupon the Russian church repudiated the Council and interpreted the fall of Constantinople in 1453 as God's just punishment to those who consorted with schismatics. To the Russians it seemed quite plain that no enemy could take the city as long as Constantinople maintained Christianity in purity and truth. But as soon as Constantinople betrayed its sacred mission, God delivered the once impregnable city to the infidel.

After 1453 Moscow came increasingly to consider itself the authentic successor of the Byzantine empire in both a secular and ecclesiastical sense. The latter was spelled out in a series of celebrated letters to Ivan III and his son Vasily III from the monk of Pskov, Filofei, who at one point stated the Third Rome doctrine in these terms:

> Of all kingdoms in the world, the Holy Apostolic
> Church shines in thy royal domain more brightly
> than the sun. So take note, thy Majesty, most
> religious and gracious Tsar, that all kingdoms of
> the Orthodox Christian Faith have been merged
> into thy kingdom. In all that lies under heaven
> thou alone art a Christian tsar. So take note, most
> religious and gracious Tsar, that all Christian king-
> doms have been merged into thine alone, for *two
> Romes have fallen, but the third still stands and a
> fourth there shall never be.* [Emphasis added.]

> Thy Christian kingdom shall not fall as inheritance
> to another.

These tenets laid grave responsibilities upon the Russian church. The obligation of the Russian state to maintain Byzantine traditions was considered equally great. An important landmark in the fusion of Byzantine tradition and the Muscovite future was the marriage of Ivan III to Zoe Paleologue in 1472. Sophia, as she was renamed in Russia, was the niece of Constantine XI, the last Byzantine emperor, who had died in the defense of Constantinople in 1453 after sending his family to safety in Rome. The Vatican hoped Sophia's marriage to Ivan would further reunification of the churches, perhaps even add Russian military power to a grand western campaign to drive the Turks from the Byzantine empire.

Sophia did nothing in Moscow to further these papal ambitions. She had long resented being treated as nothing more than an instrument of papal politics; she must also have seen that in any event she would not have been able to influence Russian policies in a direction favorable to Rome. The significance of this marriage to Ivan was simply that it linked him and his heirs to the last generation of Byzantine rulers. Whether or not Sophia was mainly responsible for this, it seems that after the 1470s Moscow was flooded with Byzantine influences: court ceremony and regalia were refashioned along Greek lines, the double-headed eagle was now more often used as the Russian symbol too, and in 1493 Ivan formally assumed the title "Sovereign of all Russia." The last point was important because a *sovereign* ruler was then considered to hold his power directly from God, not from any other man such as a Mongol khan, a Holy Roman Emperor or a Pope. After his Byzantine marriage, and after his repudiation of all obligations to the Mongols in 1480, Ivan III could even view himself as an "autocrat" (*samoderzhavets*), a word which in both its English and Russian forms indicates "one who holds power in and of himself," not one, for example, who exercises certain authority through serving another as a vassal. A tenuous and highly labored genealogy linking Ivan to

Caesar Augustus (!) even made it possible for Ivan to call himself "emperor" (the Slavonic form for "Caesar" is *tsar*), though the Russians did not attempt to make western powers recognize this superlative title for another half century.

The conviction of Muscovy that it was the historic heir of Byzantium is part of what Miliukov in the first chapter of this book terms the "nationalistic ideology" of the Muscovite state, even if it did not become a part of the Russian "national consciousness" (also Miliukov's phrase) until the later sixteenth century. Some recent research on the Third Rome doctrine has called into question Miliukov's contention that the Russian church did not lead the way in developing the national idea (even in the elaboration of ideology Miliukov saw the state as playing the main role!). Whatever the merits of these arguments, Miliukov made a particular contribution to Russian historiography on the subject through his careful analysis of South Slavic influence in the genesis of the Third Rome idea in Moscow. These pages deserve close attention.

"Ideology" as Miliukov often uses the word, might be thought of as a body of principles showing how a society should be organized and governed to serve the demands of justice. Miliukov shows that Ivan III and his associates used ideology to justify the accumulation of power by the Muscovite state. It was indeed necessary that Moscow's ascendency be vindicated to contemporaries, for in earlier times "Russia" had not been a thoroughly authoritarian state in which an absolute ruler prevailed so totally over all social classes. As late as the time of Ivan's father Vasily II (1425-1462), Moscow was but one of several independent principalities. A great landed aristocrat (boyar) probably had estates in several Russian principalities, and though he served a prince, each boyar enjoyed the theoretical right to choose *which* prince. Tradition even dictated that a boyar might "depart" the service of one prince for that of another without forfeiture of lands. This was because a boyar was a *votchinik*, the holder of a "votchina," land gained "from the father" and not held on condition of service, hence patrimonial or hereditary land which could be freely disposed of or passed on to heirs.

Ominous for the boyars was the fact that by the mid-1400s another class of aristocrats was in an advanced stage of formation. This was the class of the *pomeshchiki*, or holders of a "pomestie," a word which in Russian means literally "at my place" (*po mesto*). This "place" was quite different from a votchina. The pomestie was much smaller and was held from the prince who owned the land in return for service, usually military. Later generations of "service nobles" could expect to use their estates throughout their lives and transmit them at death to sons, who would in turn undertake the necessary service to the prince. But this was not the case in the fifteenth century. The pomestie could be taken from its holder at any time, and the early pomeshchik had no assurance that his heir (even if capable of undertaking the obligations customary for the pomestie) would receive this landholding.

The rise of Muscovite autocracy was accompanied by a shift in power from the boyars to the service nobles. The tsars fostered the latter class, using them to destroy – literally, at times – the ancient, privileged boyar families. Naturally this caused the growth of what Miliukov calls "oppositionist ideology," for the lesser princes of the house of Rurik (now deprived of their patrimonies by annexation to Moscow) joined with the boyars to resist the loss of their wealth, prestige and independence. Little wonder that Ivan the Terrible (1547-1584) found his great nobles taking advantage of early defeats in Russia's war for the Baltic to desert to Poland and Lithuania, where their social peers, the *pani*, collectively were more powerful than the king. When Prince Kurbsky deserted to the enemy and engaged in his famous polemic with Ivan between 1564 and 1579, he stated succinctly the boyar position. Kurbsky argued that Ivan's cruelty and lust released his subjects from any obligation to serve him. Oaths extracted by force are not binding, nor is a realm governed by tyranny rather than law truly a state. "When the customs of our fathers have been extinguished" the individual has the right, if not to resist, at least to flee persecution and death.

The boyars as a class never recovered from Ivan the Terrible's struggle with so many of their number. The term *boyar* continued to be used in the next century, but it then almost always referred to an entirely new group of aristocrats, men who had gained the special favor of the tsar (or his high officials at court) and whose title and position depended upon his continued good will. These "boyars" were bound to the Muscovite autocracy no less securely than the lesser pomeshchik, or "service nobleman." Moreover, by the early seventeenth century the service nobles had gained almost all the land owned by the true boyars a hundred years earlier. In this struggle the service nobles also developed an ideology. In connection with this Miliukov discusses the fascinating and enigmatic Ivan Peresvetov, the wandering mercenary and adventurer whose writings early in the reign of Ivan the Terrible warn the young tsar against his "seditious" boyars and call upon him to be a firm autocrat, to sweep treason from the land, to reward his service nobles for the fealty they could be expected to show their sovereign. If power in the land be divided, says Peresvetov, this is an "unnatural" state of affairs which will produce chaos and injustice. Such a situation could be remedied only through the monarch's decisive action.

The oppositionist ideology of the old boyars died with them; the nationalist ideology — expounded in different yet related forms by Filofei and Peresvetov — triumphed along with the autocracy. It seemed to Miliukov that the only development which could have checked the growth of the absolutist state in Russia would have been an alliance such as developed in England between the service nobles and town merchants. In his *History of Russia* Miliukov notes that these two groups formed the "foundations of the country's economic and military power," and a coalition between them might have forced the tsar to share power with them. At times the merchants were in a militant mood, determined to force the government to expel foreign competitors or to abandon certain inflationary fiscal policies.

All chances for such a development ended in 1649. In
that year a new law code was adopted which recognized
serfdom and ended the right of debt-free peasants to freedom
of movement. Legal restrictions placed on the peasantry
accomplished more than to pacify the service nobility. To the
average pomeshchik it probably now seemed that the future
of serfdom and autocracy were bound together, and that to disturb the latter would not serve his interests as a serfholder.
Nor did the wealthier merchants desire legal safeguards so much
as redress of specific grievances. Even so, the government
was able increasingly to ignore their demands. The remainder
of the seventeenth century was punctuated by urban uprisings
(Pskov in 1650 and Moscow in 1661) and peasant-Cossack
rebellions (most notably that of Stenka Razin in 1668). But
these episodes displayed a primitive, elemental character
scarcely capable of transforming society or even of overturning
the regime. It is striking that no coherent peasant ideology
of opposition emerged in this period, or at least little beyond
the grumblings of Maksim the Greek over the abuse of peasants
by their monastic lords (as if, Miliukov dryly notes, other
peasants did not merit equal sympathy!).

Sometimes the church in the West presented challenges
to the state, but nothing in the traditions of the Russian
church enabled it to function as a countervailing force to Muscovite autocracy. The established order was partially chal-
lenged in the late fifteenth century, when Nil Sorsky and
other monks demanded that the church divest itself of land
and turn from blind obedience to "corrupt" secular power and
to seek apostolic simplicity and love. But the church council
of 1503 called to debate the matter resoundingly supported the
"possessors," the monastic party led by Joseph of Volokolamsk
which emphasized the need for the church to be wealthy and
to support unconditionally a godly autocracy. Such heretics
as the Judaizers were easily rooted out and destroyed, along
with those "non-possessors" who refused to accept the decision
of 1503 and continued to call for an end to monastic privileges

and wealth. Oppositionist ideologies failed one by one in the
face of what Miliukov termed a persistent "unity of national
growth." The social and political cost of this failure was
the impressment into state service of privileged and impover-
ished alike, and their forced assumption of ever greater obligations. No social force in Russia could stop the flowering
of state power and the nationalist ideology upon which it
rested.

    This is not to say that Russia did not have its experience
with representative institutions. The Romanov dynasty
elected in 1613 entered into a forty year period of contention
with very active "Assemblies of the Land" (*zemskie sobory*).
In his *History of Russia* Miliukov notes that the zemskie sobory
from 1613 through the 1640s were elected bodies which
evolved from a consultative organ to one that "actually shared
the power of the tsar" and even "dictated its wishes to the
country." But in Russia the social forces and opposition ideologies necessary to limit autocracy permanently were not
present. In both theory and practice the absolutist character
of the government remained intact, dormant for the moment,
but waiting to be summoned again to active life by such a
person as Peter the Great.

    Miliukov saw a sharp polarity between Russia and the
West which he traced back as far as Muscovite times. The West
represented "civilization" whereas Russia was backward and
apathetic. Miliukov's sympathies lay entirely with the West
and its traditions of political democracy and individual rights.
He observed that in the West the dynamically developing
economy triggered sharp struggles between monarchies and
ruling classes. Therefore he accepted in part the Marxist
notion that social-economic relations in the West ultimately
dictated the form and ideology of government. But a chasm
separated Russia from the West, Miliukov argued, making the
Russian situation entirely different. Miliukov admitted
that the Russian state always rested upon certain social foundations and generally observed the needs of social groups with

which it was allied. He conceded that different classes had contended at various times to influence state policy. But he rejected the Marxist idea that the Russian state could be properly understood as the coercive instrument of a ruling class. Rather than the state in this sense "serving" society, Miliukov insisted that the Russian state bound *all* social classes to *its* service. Thus the evolution of state authority in Russia bore a supra-class character, and military needs and financial questions were more important than the ability of one class to dominate others through government and law.

Miliukov agreed with the Marxists that the class struggle, the struggle of the exploited against their exploiters, was a theme in the Russian past. But from his treatment of Russian history one must think that Miliukov, following Soloviev, was more impressed with another reality: the ability of the state to maintain social order — or restore it when disrupted — and to harness the energies of all *sosloviia* (social orders) to its own, independent purposes. Marx and Engels themselves may have had intuitions into this aspect of the historical process when they expressed two highly suggestive (and unfortunately unelaborated) thoughts. The class struggle in some instances can end "in the common ruin of the contending classes," and in occasional situations of class conflict, the opposing social forces so balance and neutralize each other that the state gains a momentary independence and is able to pursue lines of policy not directly related to the needs of any class. But Marxists would clearly regard such situations as exceptional and ephemeral. To Miliukov, however, this was the basic reality of Russian history: the ability of the state to keep order between classes and nationalities so that the state itself might pursue its own objectives.

Miliukov's views as here summarized present an entirely respectable (if not universally accepted) interpretation of the role of the state in Russian history from Mongol times through the eighteenth century. But Miliukov also seems to place

himself in a rather paradoxical situation. As an historian
dwelling in the world of pro-western sympathies, Miliukov
had to admire the absolutist state of Ivan the Terrible
and Peter the Great. With all its faults at least that state
was an agent of unification and "progress," a strong instrument for "westernizing" a slothful nation unable to stir to
life in any other way. On humanitarian grounds Miliukov
might deplore the bloodshed which accompanied the
Petrine reforms (actually his writings did this less and less
as years passed), but he could not challenge the validity
of the reform program as such. Yet, as a liberal who lived
in the world of struggle against the Russian autocracy of
his own time, Miliukov also had to lament the absence of
the social developments which would have made Russian
traditions more "democratic" — but which would also have
undermined the autocracy at that very moment in the
past when supposedly it acted in "progressive" fashion. Had
the Russian autocratic state been so weakened, it would
have been far less able to respond to problems involving the
interests of the entire nation, especially in the diplomatic-
military arena.

Once a Russian intellectual of Miliukov's time decided
that Russia and the West represented two significantly
different worlds, should not that person have been *extremely*
cautious in the extent to which he would demand that
"modern" Russia continue to adapt itself in the future along
western lines? Is it not possible that Russian conservatives
of the late nineteenth century had a far better case than Russian and other liberal historians have taught us to believe?
Given the size of the empire, its diverse national composition,
the entire fabric of its popular attitudes and political traditions, why should anything other than a strong — even authoritarian — state ever have been natural for Russia? The West
may point the way to the future in scientific and industrial
development. But does this mean that western political forms
and cultural values are necessarily valid anywhere save in the

West? To the extent that Miliukov and his compatriots undermined the tsarist order, did they not hasten the advent of another despotism which for a time wanted to do better, but found it had to be still more authoritarian? Ideas have consequences and people who think and who propagate ideas assume a responsibility before history. Miliukov cannot be excused from this on the basis that he meant well, no more than other figures in the Russian past who come to mind — Lenin and Trotsky, for example.

But the issues in Russian history are complex and will never be resolved. Socialism has replaced capitalism in the Russian empire. But socialism has not extinguished the old polemics, which continue in but slightly modified form. There might appear to be a complete discontinuity between the intellectuals of Miliukov's generation and those of a half-century later because the social contexts are so different. But cultural traditions and visions of national destiny do not disappear quickly, if at all. Some Soviet oppositionists of the 1960s-1970s who have no conscious affinity for Paul Miliukov or for bourgeois liberalism may in fact be struggling for a Russia strikingly similar to that hoped for by Miliukov. Certainly Slavophilism has experienced a powerful rebirth in that compelling and complex writer, Alexander Solzhenitsyn, who has revived publically — in terms which would have been thoroughly familiar to Miliukov — the entire debate over the meaning of Russia's past and future. In his celebrated open "Letter" to the Soviet leadership (1973-1974), Solzhenitsyn insisted that the West's influence on Russia, now most visible in the form of industry and ideology, has always been catastrophic because it has disrupted what is most authentic in the Russian character. Solzhenitsyn calls for many reforms in this document, but he does not urge that western Marxism be replaced by western bourgeois democracy, a system in its "final decline," lacking true ethical content because its foremost concern is the resolution of materialistic conflicts in society. Solzhenitsyn frankly acknowledges that "Russia is

authoritarian. Let it remain so," he says, "and let us no
longer try to change that." Let everything change, but not
that.

Whether latter-day interpreters of Russia's past will have more
success than Miliukov in the struggle for a better Russia is
a question held in the lists of time. What is clear today is that
they have far to go in competing with the Miliukov who
dwelt in the world of historical study and letters. His striking
insights, forceful style and deft synthesis of complex strands
of historical information seldom have been equalled and perhaps never surpassed among Russian historians. If, at least as
foreign minister in the Provisional Government, Miliukov
did not make history as well as he wrote it, we are the poorer
for that.

Joseph T. Fuhrmann

PREFACE

The American student of history has always approached the study of Russia at a disadvantage. The lack of Russian historical works in English translation has deprived interested undergraduates of the opportunity to explore the Russian past through the writings of its most eminent interpreters. Many important Russian historians have yet to find their translators. Others, such as Kliuchevsky, are known in American classrooms only through inadequate translations that destroy the vitality and often the accuracy of the original. Yet American scholars continue to neglect the task of making accessible to their students the finer fruits of Russian labors in historiography. It is hoped that this work, with my previous renditions of S. F. Platonov's *Moscow and the West* and *Ivan the Terrible*, will help fill this lacuna and encourage others to embark upon similar endeavors.

The works of Paul Miliukov pose special difficulties for the translator. Deeply involved in the political crisis of his own day, Miliukov often found detachment from his own historical milieu difficult. For this reason his accounts of early Russian history are infused with terminology and interpretations that are anachronistic to the age with which he deals. Contemporary scholars will object to his use of the terms *soslovie* and *klass* to characterize social groups that in earlier times had yet to coalesce into the class formations known in later history. In such instances I have labored to reproduce his meaning with exactness and literalness. When Miliukov speaks of the "intelligentsia" or the "bourgeoisie" of seventeenth-century Russia, however, I can merely throw up my hands in exasperation and render his thought with precision, if not with admiration and agreement.

I have striven to present Miliukov's thought with care
and fidelity, with considerations of style and usage definitely
subordinated to the former concern. I have also retained
Miliukov's italicization of important words and phrases throughout this text, despite the awareness that this practice might
annoy some readers. I have excised from this version both his
rather lengthy introduction and his bibliographical citations
accompanying each chapter, both of which strike me as dated
and of little contemporary value. By the same token I have
removed Miliukov's frequent references to the first two volumes
of his *Outlines of Russian Culture*, much of which is unavailable in a complete English translation. As with my work on
Platonov, I have attempted to keep my editorial annotations to
a minimum, identifying only those personalities and events
that receive no further elucidation in the original. This unabridged translation is taken from the first 155 pages of volume
three of Miliukov's *Ocherki po istorii russkoi kul'tury* (Paris,
1930-1937).

The system of transliteration employed is consonant with
my earlier translations. The basic Library of Congress system has been modified through omission of ligatures and the
reproduction of the endings of Russian proper names as "y,"
not as "ii." The soft sign is often suppressed in common nouns
and proper names, especially when it precedes a vowel. Russian dipthongs are given as "ya" and "yu" when beginning proper or place names. Familiar Russian names have been anglicized (such as Peter, Alexis and Michael). Non-Russian names
are retained in their national form (thus Maszkiewicz, not
Maskevich).

I must thank the Research Committee of Virginia Polytechnic Institute and State University for granting me funds that
allowed me to research background material for this and similar projects in scholarly libraries throughout the eastern United
States. Many colleagues have contributed to the success of this

effort through counsel, encouragement and simple kindness.
Among these are Professors Dimitri von Mohrenschildt,
Nicholas Riasanovsky, Richard Hellie, Robert Crummey and
Charles Schlacks, Jr. Professor Joseph T. Fuhrmann has
read the manuscripts and offered many valuable suggestions.
Professor Peter von Wahlde first launched this undertaking
by urging me to consider Miliukov as a subject worthy of
greater use in the classroom. Mrs. Wolter Fabrycky has again
shared with me her unique knowledge of the early Russian
language and has doggedly pursued some of the more archaic
terms in Miliukov's work. Errors that remain are mine alone.

 As ever, my wife, Jo, has contributed more to this work
than all others. In dedicating this book to her I attempt to
convey paltry thanks to one whose contribution to my work
is ineffable.

Joseph L. Wieczynski

Virginia Polytechnic Institute and State University
February, 1974

The Origins of Ideology

I

THE RISE OF MOSCOW AND MUSCOVITE IDEOLOGY

The last twenty years of the fifteenth century in Russian history
are remarkable for a number of innovations that sharply distinguish these years from all previous times. Russian political life
abruptly entered upon a new path. Instead of a number of
principalities, divided into a multiplicity of small appanages,
we now encounter a consolidated unit of Muscovite domains,
which was already devouring almost all the lands of its neighbors,
large and small alike. In place of the former grand prince, we
now see the "Sovereign of All Rus."[1] This sovereign was now
concerned not with petty purchases of land and "newly acquired
properties," but with the final unification of all the Russian
people under his own authority. To achieve this goal he no
longer endeavored to bribe the advisers of the Khan or to
pester the Khan for the yarlyk.[2] Now he himself was a "Tsar,"
in no way inferior to the ruler of the Horde, and an "autocrat"
whose power did not depend upon foreign sanction of any
sort. His diplomats wished to be on equal footing in all instances
not only with the government of the Republic of Venice but
with the Holy Roman Emperor himself. In short, because of
the spontaneous successes achieved by his "ancestors," the
Muscovite sovereign elaborated a broad political program to
which his government and his successors consciously and firmly
adhered in the future. But what is especially interesting here,
current problems of state first received a more or less abstract
ideological formulation as part of this program. The political
ideology of the Muscovite state program quickly became part
of the "popular consciousness" and long survived the historical

circumstances that had created that ideology. For this reason
this program must be treated with particular attention; its
practical elements must be distinguished carefully from those
that were ideological.

One might think that it was precisely the latter, that is,
the ideological elements, that appeared such an innovation as
to impart an unusual and striking tint to the entire period
during which the new political program was implemented.
But on the contrary, the elements that arose directly from
the needs of current life linked Muscovite reality with the
past and were merely the direct and logical result of the slow
and spontaneous work of previous generations. Let us attempt
to analyze both component parts of the Muscovite political
program.

The "spontaneous work" of the ancestors of the Muscovite
autocrat undoubtedly contained its own consciousness and
tradition. Simeon the Proud, the son of Kalita,[3] stressed this
tradition with full clarity as early as 1353 when he concluded
his last testament with the following expression: "But I write
you this word so that the memory of our parents and our own
memory will not cease, and *the candle shall not be extinguished.*"
Simeon could have been tranquil on this point. The candle lit
by Kalita did not go out, but flared up with bright flames in
the days of his sons, grandsons, great-grandsons and great-great-
grandsons. The first Russian autocrat stood upon the shoulders
of five generations; for this reason he was able to see so far and
wide. It is also true, however, that his ancestors had never
dreamed of such broad prospects. Buying up and annexing
village after village and volost after volost,[4] accumulating in
their treasury gold and silver, necklaces and neckpieces, jackets
studded with pearls and belts with stones, cheating the Tatars
of tribute and doing violence to the princes who were their
own brothers, these ancestors had no greater political dream
than the vague hope that some day would come when "God
would free them from the Horde." If asked what they would
do with their freedom, probably they could not have

developed any program beyond their old, customary, instinctive practice of annexing and accumulating, cheating and committing acts of violence, with the sole purpose of acquiring as much power and money as possible. Thus the tradition of thrift was the most fundamental, most natural and least ideological of all the traditions of the Muscovite grand princely family.

The need to struggle against the Tatars, it is true, gave rise to other goals that were more abstract. But these goals were hardly perceived clearly, especially because they contradicted in part the usual problems of practical politics. Directly before the words already cited from Simeon's testament are found counsels which, although traditional, contain a very practical implication. "Just as my father has commanded that you live as one, so I also command you. Do not heed evil people, and if anyone quarrels with you, listen to our father, Bishop Alexis."[5] The necessity to be "as one" was indeed very sensible in light of the prospective struggle with the Tatars. Yet such unity could only be achieved in practice at the cost of one rival destroying all the rest. Thus this "ancestral" moral necessarily assumed a different form when it came from the lips of a happy victor. The victor no longer needed to be "as one," for he remembered full well that there was no need to share with others. The force of circumstances had transformed the old Russian tradition of "unity" (which derived from the Kievan South) into the tradition of "unification." Not the uniting of kindred princes, but the unity of power in the hands of a single "sovereign" — this was the practical lesson the Prince of Moscow learned from the futility of his great-grandfather's moral.

By a happy accident we know from Ivan III's own pronouncements how clearly and consciously he learned this lesson. Alexander, the Lithuanian prince who had married Ivan's daughter, Elena, wished to give his brother, Sigismund, an appanage[6] in the Lithuanian land. This news raised in Ivan's mind a whole host of recollections, and he dictated to his ambassador, who was going to Elena at Vilna, the following impressive warning: "It has been communicated to me that the Grand Prince and the Pani[7] wish to give Sigismund Kiev and other towns in the Grand Principality of Lithuania. Is that so, my daughter! I have heard what discord there was in the Lithuanian land when there were many sovereigns. And you have also heard what discord there was in our land during my father's time.[8] And I hope that you also recall how things were between me and my brother after my father's death.[9] If Sigismund should be in the Lithuanian land, how will you benefit from this? I order that this be transmitted to you because you are our child and because your affairs are beginning to proceed improperly, for which I am sorry."

Ivan did conduct his "affairs properly," but he was not entirely true to his forefathers. As time passed, these forefathers ever more often accompanied the counsels that we have already seen — to be as one "with one's brother" — with decrees that reduced the moral obligation of the younger brothers to political necessity. "Ivan's ancestors" ever increasingly enlarged the share of inheritance for the eldest and deprived the younger of their just portion. It is well known that the oldest son of Dmitry Donskoi paid 34 per cent of the tribute given the Tatars from his own inherited share, which meant that he was master of one third of all income in Russia. His great-grandson, Ivan III, received from his father half of all Russian towns, and the best ones at that. Ivan passed on to his son a share that accounted for fully 72 per cent of the Tatar tribute, that is, almost three quarters of all Russian revenue.

Therefore, when Ivan III criticized the policies of his forefathers, he did so with the hindsight provided by the results of these policies. Ivan merely saw better and farther, and hence could deal with their idea much more consciously. Above all, however, obstacles to the realization of this idea were so weakened by Ivan's day that he enjoyed the full opportunity to implement this notion with incomparable consistency.

Simeon's testament contains one additional counsel, besides that on moral unity, the influence of which has just been traced. "Listen to Bishop Alexis," Simeon wrote. This advice indicates another noteworthy element that played a role in the new political ideology, that of religion. By its very nature, religion seems to have given even a more forceful impetus to ideology than did political struggle. It is also obvious that Muscovite politics fashioned religion into an instrument primarily to attain immediate, practical objectives.

The struggle of the new political centers over which would become the residence of the metropolitan began, as is known, from very early times. The metropolitan was the religious representative of "*all* Rus" long before the Prince of Moscow became its political representative. Through his very position the metropolitan was the official representative of all the Russian people as long as all Rus remained the sole eastern Slavic diocese under the Patriarch of Constantinople. Moreover, the metropolitan was more than an unintentional representative of "all Rus;" he also transferred this position to the prince whose principality he chose for his permanent residence. When the Prince of Tver, Mikhail Yaroslavich, succeeded in securing the favor of Metropolitan Peter,[10] he immediately began to call himself "Grand Prince of *All Rus,*" in imitation of the metropolitan's title. In like manner the Muscovite rival to the princes of Tver, Ivan Kalita, introduced nothing new but simply copied his enemies when, having won Metropolitan Peter to his side, he also adopted that same title, "Grand Prince of All Rus." It must be remembered that both events occurred a century and a half before Ivan III founded his own national politics upon the use of this title.

But nothing similar to Ivan's policies can be found among those who preceded him in using this title. This point of comparison alone indicates that during the fourteenth century the religious element was still unable to play the political role that it assumed from the end of the fifteenth century. Obviously the notion of all-Russian religious unity did not conjure up the idea of all-Russian political unity, and even the title of Grand Prince "of all Rus" sounded completely harmless and innocent. At best it registered pretensions to hegemony over the particular political federation that had represented the system of principalities during the appanage period, and not at all the aspiration for political unification of the entire Russian people.

The Church had already played out its ancient role as the representative of spiritual unity by the time that Ivan III initiated his unifying policies. No longer could the Church serve as the bearer of the national idea, for by that time the Church itself had suffered division into two halves that corresponded to the two parts of Rus, Lithuanian and Muscovite. In the middle of the century Lithuanian Rus received its own spiritual head. He followed in the footsteps of Metropolitan Isidore by striving to implement formal recognition of the Florentine Union by the southwestern Russian Church.[11] Conversely, from that same moment the diocese of northeastern Rus became fully subordinated to the objectives of princely politics and, by sacrificing its freedom and independence from secular authority, won its independence from the Byzantine Patriarch, at first in practice, then later formally as well. In this instance the Church did not lead the way for the national idea but served its development as an obedient instrument in the hands of the government.

This instrument was first used extensively in the 1480s and 1490s. The sovereign of "all Rus" declared war on the sovereign of Lithuania in the name of defending Orthodoxy against the "Roman law." He justified all his seizures of Lithuanian territory by the defense of Orthodoxy, a justification employed not only with his immediate neighbor, but with other sovereigns of Europe and the Pope as well. Here was a case of ideology confronting reality, yet failing to coincide fully with reality. Lithuanian Rus had its own Orthodox party that fought against the Catholicization of Lithuania. But this group conducted its struggle by quite different means and was so undesirous of Ivan's assistance that, in the final analysis, he failed to consider initiating closer relations with it. For Ivan's immediate goals it sufficed to have a constant pretext for interference in Lithuanian affairs. This pretext was afforded him by his daughter's oppression by Catholics (which was largely imaginary). One merely has to read the constant reproaches to his son-in-law and the reprimands to his daughter in the diplomatic papers of this period to understand how all these discourses finally became a formula of excellent use to Muscovite diplomats, even if it totally disregarded reality. Ivan further explained that the incorporation into his service of petty princes along the border and the transfer of their holdings to Moscow was likewise "necessary, that they be prevented from coming under the Roman law."

Thus it is apparent that the politics of unification and the use of the national-religious idea in support of these politics were both rooted in the more or less distant past, in the politics of the forerunners of the Muscovite autocrat. Yet these ancient ideas, as employed by Ivan III, were enriched with new features and in the end completely lost their former character. Hence, the notion of the moral unity of all "brothers" succumbed to the unconditional political subordination of all others to the "eldest," as their "master." The idea of the religious unity of all the Russian people also served as a justification for the aggressive policies of the Prince of Moscow. Both changes could have been accomplished (and to some extent were) simply through changing circumstances, without the influence of extraneous ideologies. But now we must direct our attention to the other side of this question, to the purely ideological element in the Muscovite program. Analysis of this element will explain why the new program was formulated so expeditiously and consciously, and whence originated the ideological features of this program, with which we have yet to become acquainted.

II

EUROPE DISCOVERS MUSCOVY

The reason for the rapid ideological metamorphosis that clothed the grand prince of the appanage period in the costume of the Tsar can be discovered precisely where it was two centuries later, when the Muscovite Tsar adopted European dress. During Peter's day Russia was interested in Europe and began to ladle out full handfuls of new customs and ideas from Europe's cultural treasure-house. During Ivan III's day, Muscovite Rus was still too uncultured to become interested in Europe. But Europe was now becoming interested in Russia and sowed on Russian soil tiny seeds which, in that virgin soil, quickly put forth highly original shoots.

During the era of Ivan III all of educated Europe was obsessed with a single idea, that of a general crusade against the Turks. With the exception of Belgrade, which remained under the Hungarians until 1521, the Balkan Peninsula was already in Turkish hands by the last decades of the fifteenth century. From the Danube the Turks threatened the Rumanians and the Hungarians, the Austrian Slavs and the Germans. They also had begun to look attentively toward Italy, where more than once they had been lured by the internal quarrels of petty dynasties. By then all these lands had felt the power of Turkish forays. The natural leader of opposition to the triumph of Islam was the head of the western Christian world, the Pope. In addition to the Pope, Italy had two parties that were most interested in this struggle — Genoa and Venice. These commercial republics were rivals in southeastern Europe and had their colonies throughout that area. Outside of Italy interested parties included the descendants of the last Byzantine Emperor (who were selling their rights to whoever offered them the best price[1]) and the Holy Roman Emperor of the Germans, who was trying to fish in the troubled waters of European politics for the best possible catch along his eastern border. All these individuals and governments shared too many egotistical motives and contradictory interests to offer much hope for the creation of an ideological union. Hence, they accorded honor and rank all the more readily to anyone who would agree to participate disinterestedly in such a union.

At this moment in history Europe discovered Russia. The honor for this discovery belongs largely to the inhabitants of the Levant. The Levanter, a man without a homeland, keen of mind but loose in morals, who readily balanced himself on that imperceptible boundary separating diplomacy from charlatanism, had undoubtedly come into existence by that time. Observant and shrewd, such people knew how to divine who needed what and traded in goods for which there was demand. In Italy they opened academies of poetry and interpreted Homer and Demosthenes. In Moscow they proposed to the grand prince that he take in marriage the niece of the Byzantine Emperor, Zoe (Sophia) Paleologos. This was ticklish business, for the Pope thought Zoe, whom he had sheltered,[2] to be a zealous Catholic, while the Muscovite prince required "an Orthodox Christian woman." Two Levanters, one an Italian, the other a Greek, removed this obstacle in the best way possible. The Italian, Gian-Battista della Volpe, who headed Ivan's mint, took it upon himself to deceive the Pope by promising him that Russia would submit to the Holy See. The Greek was Yury Trakhaniot, the *magister domus* or steward of the bride's father, Thomas Paleologos, who had joined the Muscovite service. Trakhaniot deceived Ivan III by testifying, supposedly in the name of the Byzantine cardinal, Bessarion,[3] to Zoe's "Orthodox Christianity" and recounting in addition a mass of fables concerning her suitors, whom she was said to have spurned out of her repugnance toward Latinism (though in truth these suitors had spurned her). While en route, the messenger Volpe was also able to trick the Venetians, enticing them with the prospect of an alliance with the Golden Horde and proposing himself as their agent. The latter bit of business miscarried, but the former enterprise prospered. The Muscovite "barbarian" became the husband of the "Byzantine Princess," as the Catholic Zoe never ceased calling herself, even after she became the Orthodox Sophia on Russian soil in 1472.

Was Ivan III clearly aware of all the advantages that were now his in the eyes of Europe because of this marriage? For its part, Europe missed no opportunity to remind him of these advantages. Ivan had now won the right to enter the family of civilized European sovereigns in the honorable role of defender of Christianity against the Turks, a role which, as we have seen, had especially interested Europe earlier. For this reason as early as 1473 the Venetian Senate reminded Ivan that "in the event that the male line of the Byzantine Emperors terminates, the hereditary rights pass to him, Ivan, through his wife." The heir to these rights personally appeared in Moscow in 1480 and again in 1490, ready to sell these rights for money. The thrifty Prince of Moscow probably did not find these rights worth the asking price, and Andrew Paleologos found a more remunerative buyer in the person of the French king, Charles VIII.

But the Muscovite sovereign also had to have certain definite status in the ruling family of Europe. And so attempts were launched to purchase from Ivan his services at the price of a kingly title. As early as 1484 Pope Sixtus IV hastened to calm the alarm of the Polish king, Casimir, on this point. The Pope informed Casimir that, should Ivan ask the Pope for the title of emperor or king "of the entire Russian nation" (*in tota ruthenica natione*), he would not grant him this title without first asking the permission of the Poles. These Polish

fears were also known by a German who chanced to travel to
Russia in 1486, Nicholas Poppel.[4] According to the information that Poppel communicated to the grand prince in Moscow
over the course of two years, "the King of Poland is very
desirous that the Roman Pope not make the Grand Prince a
king. He has sent great gifts to the Pope, so the Pope will not
do this . . . . The Poles very much fear that, should Your
Grace be king, then *all the Russian land that is under the
Polish king will be lost to him and will obey Your Grace.*"

Here, as in our own day, "too much care for the patient
became the cause of the illness." The Prince of Moscow
indifferently heard out Poppel's assurances that this was not
the Pope's concern, that only the Emperor could confer the
title of king and that Ivan could, if he wished, receive this
title under certain conditions from Poppel's master. The
great name of the "Roman Emperor" was but an empty
sound to the ignorant ears of Ivan III. The title of king not
only left him completely indifferent but even, as a sign of
some sort of subordination, annoyed him. Having become a
member of the European family, Ivan wished to be first or,
if this were impossible, to remain as he was, not at all bound
by the established hierarchy of European sovereigns.

The first Muscovite ambassadors refused to yield in
honor to France or Spain, then the most powerful states of
Europe. In the Cathedral of Saint Mark and in the Court of
the Vatican they claimed first place. In Vienna they demanded
that the Emperor nominate his own heir as the fiance of the
daughter of the Prince of Moscow, for dukes and margraves
were too insignificant for her.[5] The most astute political wisdom could not have dictated to Ivan a more adroit answer
than that which he gave Poppel from his naive ignorance of
European relations. "Why did you speak to us of kingship,"
the diplomats of the Prince of Moscow replied to the German
ambassador, "when we, by the grace of God, are sovereigns
in our land from the beginning, since the first of our ancestors;
and we have this appointment from God, as did our ancestors.

And we ask God to grant that we and our children will abide forever in this manner, as sovereigns in our own land. Just as we did not desire an appointment by anyone in the past, so now also we do not desire it." This sort of justification, however, which was prompted by the old tradition of practicality, was found to be inadequate even in Moscow. A few months later Muscovite ambassadors invented for the Emperor a new and more magnificent reply in which, as we shall see, a political ideology imported from abroad now played a role.

Be this as it may, Ivan III remained cold to the temptations of western political law. But he reacted quite differently to the idea of "pan-Russianism," as suggested to him by Poppel. We do not know how well grounded had been the fears of the Polish king. But even if Ivan III had not previously hit upon the idea of using Lithuanian Rus as a weapon, the reminders and hints that now came to him from abroad must have impressed him deeply. Was it really possible to procure "the entire Russian land, which was under the Polish king (and the Grand Prince of Lithuania)" even *without* the title of king and without the sanction of the Pope or the Emperor? The answer to this question can be found in the words just cited, as told to Poppel by Muscovite diplomats. If Muscovites had forgotten that southern Rus had also belonged at one time to the Grand Prince of Kiev (who could also be regarded an "ancestor" and his holdings a Muscovite "patrimony"), now the Emperor and the Pope were to remind them of this fact. For this reason Ivan, having rejected the title of king, energetically seized upon the hints made to him concerning his possible claim to possess all Rus. In 1490 he answered the Emperor's ambassador, Georg von Thurn, that he desired love and friendship and "unity" with the "king," Maximilian, and that he was prepared "to be at one with him against his enemies," that is, against the King of Poland. Then they could both "secure their patrimonies" from their mutual rival: the Kingdom of Hungary for Maximilian and the "Grand Principality of Kiev" for Ivan. Ivan then pressed the Emperor, reproaching him for his lack of ardor and trying to convince him "to put aside your other affairs and to adhere strictly to your concerns here."

When assistance from Maximilian was not forthcoming, Ivan finally resolved to act himself and did so with stubborn persistence, startling foreign observers and winning his desired objective. In 1493 he formally adopted the title suggested to him by historical precedent and refreshed in his memory so opportunely by the diplomats of the Pope and the Emperor, the title of "Sovereign of All Rus." The protest of his Lithuanian son-in-law, who held sway over half of this "all Rus" was answered by Muscovite diplomats with an assurance and self-confidence that were to remain their prerogatives long thereafter: "Our Sovereign has written nothing that is lofty and has introduced nothing new. From the beginning he has been the rightful *native sovereign* of all Rus, which God has bestowed upon him from his grandfathers and great-grandfathers."

With every peaceful usurpation and military acquisition Ivan successively developed this newly adopted viewpoint. Everything taken from Lithuania was "our patrimony." "There is nothing that we now have that is not our patrimony," Muscovites did not forget to add on each occasion, "and all the Russian land, by God's will, is our patrimony from olden times through our ancestors." In 1504, one year before Ivan's death, this thesis received still greater definition: "All the Russian land — Kiev, Smolensk and other towns — is our patrimony from our ancestors, and he (the king) should surrender to us the *entire* Russian land: Kiev, Smolensk and *other towns*." This vague reference to "other" towns enabled one to expand his claims unceasingly. Thus in 1517, during the reign of Vasily III, we encounter the formula, "Kiev, *Polotsk, Vitebsk*" and once again, "other towns." Even the most composed reader of these dry ambassadorial reports can feel the heavy, measured tread of the Muscovite "Stone Guest," as if in an oppressive nightmare.

But what became of the grand prince's mission as the defender of Christianity against "unbelievers?" In this respect the new ally disappointed western Christendom just as much as its own adherents had disappointed each other. Ivan III was different only in that he felt no need and did not trouble to conceal with high-flown phrases the egotistical lining of his politics. He had no objection to combatting paganism; but he always asked himself prudently, "*which* paganism?" Like the sovereigns of Europe and the King and Prince of Lithuania-Poland, Ivan had his own "paganism," which he befriended not only against other "paganism" but also against his Christian neighbors. One such was his old friend, Mengli-Girey,[6] the Khan of the Crimea, who had rendered Ivan indispensable services in his struggle against the Golden Horde and the Polish-Lithuanian state.

The Crimean Khan became a vassal of the Turkish Sultan at the very moment that the Sultan had ejected the Genoese from the southern coast of the Crimea. Ivan's friendship with Mengli-Girey paved the way for direct relations with the Padishah himself. After preliminary correspondence through this Crimean friend, a Muscovite envoy appeared on the shores of the Bosphorus in 1494. In the capital of the leader of these Islamic true believers, as in the capital of the Roman Emperor, the representative of the Prince of Moscow ignored established customs of etiquette and demanded exclusive status for himself. The descendant of the Prophet was severely shocked. But this did not prevent the Sublime Porte from sending to Moscow a reply, replete in the eastern manner with the most exquisite compliments, or from giving Russian merchants considerable trading advantages in 1499. Several years later, in 1503, in response to a new proposal that he conclude peace with the Polish-Lithuanian state for the sake of a general war against the Turks, Ivan III with hard words again obstinately answered the Pope that "just as he had stood for Christianity against paganism in the past, so now and henceforth,

God willing, he wishes to stand for Christianity against paganism." In the war with Lithuania, however, his enemy, and not he, was at fault, for "the Russian land of our ancestors, as of old, is our patrimony."

This was the sole ideology that Ivan III derived *directly* from his dealings with western European diplomats. But the very existence of these dealings necessarily served as the source of other ideologies and, most of all, of the further development of that just mentioned. To trace the further development of Russian national ideology we must turn from Europe to Moscow, which by this time had been enriched by the fruits of its first encounters with Europe.

III

MUSCOVY AND THE SOUTH SLAVS

The Italians and Greeks were the people most likely to establish relations between Russia and Europe. But they exerted little influence upon the Russian national psychology. The Greeks had a national patriotism that was narrow and exclusive; it had driven an insurmountable barrier between what was their own and what was foreign. Even today they have not changed their old habit of considering Russians "barbarians." One can imagine how they had acted at the time of Ivan III. Forced to flatter and bow and scrape while they solicited doles from the Muscovite sovereign, they harbored in their soul disdain and ill will toward their savage patrons. The Muscovites repaid these feelings with suspicion and mistrust. But the South Slavs felt incomparably closer to the Russians. Now they appeared as the most natural tutors of Russian national sentiment as soon as this sentiment first found expression.

The history of the South Slavs had fostered national sentiment and periodically intensified this sentiment. The cause of this intensification always was the enmity the South Slavs felt toward the Greeks. Whenever any sort of independent cultural movement arose among the Balkan Slavs, that movement was always founded upon hatred for the civilization of the "Romans," or to be more exact, of their displays of national arrogance. The objective of these national movements was always the political drive toward independence from the Byzantine Emperor and the campaign for religious independence from the Patriarch of Constantinople. Their own Slavic emperor and their own Patriarch — these were the eternal ideals that fed the national aspirations of the South Slavs.

The last time this national feeling erupted prior to the Turkish conquest was during the fourteenth century, at the time of the Bulgar, Alexander,[1] and the Serb, Dušan.[2] Both cherished the thought of conquering Constantinople and replacing Byzantium with Slavic states, one Serbian-Greek, the other Bulgarian-Greek. To begin, both began to style themselves "Tsars" and "Autocrats," and Stefan Dušan was even formally so crowned in 1346. As for ecclesiastical independence, Bulgaria had long enjoyed an independent Patriarchate, first in Ochrida, later in Trnovo. Now Dušan established for himself an independent Patriarch among the Serbs. Byzantine etiquette was copiously introduced at the courts of Slavic sovereigns who long before had grown accustomed to honoring themselves with Byzantine court titles and surrounding themselves with the outward forms of honor accepted at the Byzantine imperial court.

The political program of Moscow, the new heiress of Constantinople, was in its main particulars suggested by precedents among the South Slavs. Then and there the ideology that suited Moscow's new situation was also suggested.

A mid-fourteenth century Bulgarian manuscript, written at the command of "Tsar and Autocrat" John Alexander, contains not only the same thoughts that we find in Moscow a century and a half later, but even the very same expressions. Its author inserts into the text of an old Byzantine chronicle (that of Manasses[3]) this new paragraph: "All this happened in *old* Rome; but our new *Tsargrad* [Constantinople] stands and grows, becomes strong and is rejuvenated. Let it grow to the end, O Tsar who reigns over all, and take [upon Yourself] such a radiant and brilliant Tsar, the great Sovereign who has descended from the root of Asen,[4] the most elegant Tsar of the Bulgars. I have in mind Alexander, the most gentle and gracious and most loving, the benefactor of beggars, the great Tsar of the Bulgars, whose power is reckoned like countless suns." Here this "New Tsargrad" signified the Bulgarian capital of John Alexander, the repeatedly celebrated and most glorious town of Trnovo.

The blaring sounds that proclaimed the national grandeur of the "Tsar" and his capital, however, were interrupted at times by peals of Turkish thunder, distant at first, then growing closer. At first this did not disturb the theme of this national hymn but merely brought it new accompaniment that was at times joyful and solemn, at other times mystical and somber. Earlier national legends had represented the Slavic Tsar as the restorer of universal peace and prosperity. Now for the first time he was compared to Alexander of Macedon, his namesake, and ancient prophecies were applied to him. During his reign there will come forth from the mountains the people Alexander had restrained: Gog and Magog (who can be seen as the Turks). No one will be able to resist them; but the Lord will send an archstrategist who will slaughter them all; and soon will follow the advent of the anti-Christ and the end of the world.

Little by little events destroyed these South Slavic hopes and their eschatology. Above all, the expectations of the Bulgarian copyist of Manasses were unrealized. "New Tsargrad"

did not stand "to the end." The Turks came and seized it.
Both "New" and "Old" Tsargrad shared the fate of "old
Rome." Outraged national feeling could not, of course, be
reconciled to such a deplorable outcome. Despairing of the
possibility of triumphing through their own resources, the
South Slavic intelligentsia transferred their hopes to neighboring sovereigns whose turn to struggle against the Turks
followed that of the Balkan Peninsula. Balkan poets and
politicians, diplomats and ecclesiastics placed their hopes
first upon the Hungarians, then upon the Poles. But as
time passed these hopes came to ruin, as had the dreams
of a national Slavic state. The Balkan Slavs found their
immediate neighbors unable to help them. Thereupon
zealous patriots began to seek assistance farther away, in
the North of Europe. Moscow, which was then enigmatic
and poorly known, necessarily assumed the role that once
was destined for the capital city of Trnovo. The Muscovite
prince, who was of the same ethnic origin and faith, replaced
the national "Tsar and Autocrat" and the "handsome victor,"
something that was beyond the power of sovereigns of more
immediate countries. Services were not expected of him;
rather, ancient prophecies were now conveyed to him, prophecies that invested him with the halo of "the sole Orthodox
Tsar in the entire universe," while Moscow became the "New
Tsargrad" and the "Third Rome." All this aroused in Muscovites for the first time a more conscious national sentiment.

There was no paucity of intermediaries between Moscow
and Trnovo. Even in the fourteenth century, the era when
national consciousness first flourished in the Balkan Peninsula,
distant echoes of this Slavic movement had penetrated Muscovy
and exerted some influence. Foisted upon the Muscovite prince
from Constantinople, the Bulgarian Metropolitan Cyprian, who
was twice driven from Moscow by supporters of Muscovite
independence, finally was reconciled with Vasily I and devoted
the remainder of his days to the work that the creators of
Muscovy, Peter and Alexis,[5] had made their own. Cyprian

was the first to employ the literary style cultivated in the
Bulgarian town of Trnovo by the famous Euthymius[6] and
to use this style to exalt the memory of the metropolitan
who had been Kalita's collaborator. The unpretentious,
reserved style of former "copiers" of the lives of the saints
had not allowed wild fantasy. But now, through this new
literary style of ecclesiastical ornateness borrowed from
Byzantium by the South Slavs, national legend gained broad
access to religious literature. Thus the Muscovite princes
received a new and powerful means of propagating their
novel religious and political ideology.

In an example from the "life" of Metropolitan Peter,
Cyprian showed Muscovites how this could be done. The
earlier Russian biographer, Prokhor, had spoken of Moscow
as "a town of *honorable meekness*." Under Cyprian's pen
this expression became "*a renowned town*, called Moscow."
He also incorporated into Peter's life the famous legend
according to which the future role of the "renowned town"
was foreseen by a chance guest of Kalita. "If you listen to
me," Metropolitan Peter allegedly said to Kalita, "and build
a temple to the most pure Mother of God, then you will be
glorified above other princes; and your sons and grandsons
and your town will be renowned; and saints will begin to
live in it; and it will subordinate to itself all other towns."

After the fall of Constantinople and especially after
losing faith in their immediate neighbors (in the second half
of the fifteenth century), South Slavs appeared in Russia in
great number. They dared to follow in the footsteps of
their famous bishop and countryman by creating specific
elements of the national legend and introducing them into
literature as tendentious insertions or entire narratives.
Until modern times this literary work by the South Slavs
has remained anonymous; only in our day have these
unknown authors been revealed. To the extent that this
information can be determined, some understanding can be
gained of the origin of the entire complex of ideas that flowed

into Russian political literature in an appreciable stream at the end of the fifteenth and beginning of the sixteenth century or, better, that first created political literature in Rus.

This process began, of course, when the Muscovite prince adapted conceptions and ideas that had been developed in relation to the South Slavic sovereigns. Anticipating the course of events, first the South Slavic clergy, then the Russian clergy unceremoniously began to style the prince "Tsar," heartily garnishing their salutations to him with every possible epithet of South Slavic origin. He was "crowned by God;" he was "noble," the "lord and master," a "great power" who was "descended from God and hastened the truth," the "royal source of power," and so forth. Modern research has shown that one of these spiritual writers was none other than the famous fifteenth-century "copier of lives" who imitated the style of Euthymius of Trnovo: Pakhomy the Serb. Pakhomy even placed on the lips of the Greek Tsar, John Paleologos, recognition of the royal title of the Muscovite sovereign, as well as an explanation of why he does not yet bear this title officially. According to this imaginary statement, supposedly made by the Byzantine Emperor before the Council of Florence, Moscow preserves "greater Orthodoxy" and "higher Christianity." Only "from humility and through the majesty of his reason" is the Prince of Moscow "called not Tsar, but the Russian Grand Prince."

Thereafter all predictions and prophecies once applied to the Bulgarian John Alexander were referred to the Muscovite princes. The *"Rusyi family"* which, according to Greek traditions, was destined to conquer the Ishmaelites[7] and finally take possession of the seven hills of Tsargrad was now changed to the *"Russkii* [Russian] family."[8] "If all the signs foretold by Methodius of Olympos and Leo the Wise[9] concerning this town were realized," the Russian reader could learn, "then the last days have not yet come to pass, but will soon be realized; for it is written: The Russian family will conquer all Ishmaelites and will take the City of the

Seven Hills and therein will be enthroned." Here was the spelling mistake that gave rise to Russia's "historical mission" in regard to St. Sophia of Tsargrad.[10] Such a legend obviously would have a stronger effect upon the minds of the public at large than did recognition by the Venetian Senate or Sophia Paleologos bartering the title of her uncle, facts that were known only to the court and to diplomats.

But biding one's time in realizing these legendary or legal rights to Constantinople did not enter the calculations of Muscovite politics, especially since legend customarily linked this event with the end of the world (then expected to occur at the end of the fifteenth century). With his usual practicality the Prince of Moscow was quick to discount any long-term note and to place his earnings in circulation immediately. The reflection of St. Sophia fell upon Moscow and invested the town with a new radiance at home and abroad. The clergy, inspired by the ideas of the South Slavs, were the first to take this new path.

IV

MOSCOW, THE THIRD ROME

We have seen how a Bulgarian writer of the mid-fourteenth century endeavored to transfer the glory of "old Rome" and "old Tsargrad" to "new Tsargrad," which was Trnovo. Now this beautiful metaphor, which encompassed an entire schema of history and a complete philosophy of universal history, was effortlessly applied to Moscow. The world did not end in its seven thousandth year since creation.[1] On the contrary, with the beginning of the eighth millenium

in 1492 a new period of world history was born, a period
characterized by the name of Moscow. This notion was first
developed in Russian literature as part of a work composed
during this most crucial year. Its goal was to dispel the
fears that had been widespread among the public in antici-
pation of the end of the world. The work was the *Paskhaliia*
for eight thousand years, composed by Metropolitan Zosima.[2]
"Tsar Constantine created a new Rome, Tsargrad," Zosima
observed. But the Sovereign and Autocrat of all Rus, Ivan
Vasilievich, "the new Tsar Constantine," founded "a new
city of Constantine, Moscow."

   As if to underscore the South Slavic origin of these
notions, another Russian author, the famous monk of Pskov,
Filofei,[3] expressed these ideas openly by using the formula
previously cited from the works of Euthymius of Trnovo. In
1511 the Tsar's state secretary, Munekhin,[4] introduced to
Pskov a novelty from Moscow, the "Chronograph," an outline
of South Slavic history and its connection with the history
of Byzantium and Russia. This work had been composed for
the Russian public in 1442 by someone already discussed,
Pakhomy the Serb, the copier of the lives of the saints and
Euthymius of Trnovo's pupil. Filofei decided to alter this
chronograph for his fellow natives of Pskov and, having
completed this modification in 1512, appended his own
conclusion. He intended this resumé to emphasize the main
philosophical and historical conclusions a reader would draw
after reading the historical data which the Serb had selected
and completed before the fall of Tsargrad. Here is his conclusion, which unites ancient prophecies and new dreams in
a single statement: "The Orthodox cherish the hope that,
after enough punishment, the omnipotent Lord will again
enkindle amid evil powers the spark of righteousness, which
has been buried there as though in ashes, and will burn like
thorns the evil kingdoms of the Ishmaelites; and the light of
righteousness will shine again, and He will again establish
righteousness and an Orthodox Tsar. For all these devout

kingdoms (which the Chronograph recorded) — the Greek and
the Serbian, the Bosnian and Albanian and others — were
because of our sins allowed by God to be imprisoned by the
Godless Turks and brought to desolation and subdued to their
power. But by the grace of God and the prayers of the most
pure Mother of God and all the holy wonder-workers, our
Russian land grows, is young and is elevated. Let it grow, O
merciful Christ, let it be young and extend to the end of time.''

Not content with this exposition of his political creed
through the Chronograph, Filofei went on to propagate his
new teachings in earnest and developed them in a series of
epistles. In 1517 he wrote an epistle to the above-mentioned
Misiur Munekhin, one of the most prominent educated men
of his day. Misiur Munekhin had journeyed to the Orthodox
East about 1493 and through this journey had been drawn
into the circle of new ideas. Filofei also wrote to the grand
prince between 1514 and 1521. In his epistles he particularly
emphasized the notion that the political collapse of Orthodox
kingdoms is connected with their religious faithlessness and
that the political supremacy of Muscovy is a consequence of
its religious steadfastness. "Ninety years have passed since
the Greek kingdom was brought to ruin," he wrote to
Munekhin, "and it will not rise again, for the Greeks have
betrayed their Orthodox faith for Latinism."

In like manner, "all Christian kingdoms have come
to an end and have been summed up in the one kingdom of
our Sovereign, in the *Russian* kingdom, as the prophetical
books have foretold." And there will be no end to this
"present Orthodox kingdom of our most radiant and most
eminent Sovereign, the sole Tsar for Christians in all the
world," just as there will be no end to Orthodoxy upon
earth. "He necessarily is the sole surviving preserver of
the holy and divine altars of the holy and universal Church."
The representative of this Church is not "that of Rome or
Constantinople, but the Church of the Holy and Glorious
Assumption of the Mother of God in the city of Moscow,

which has been saved by God and which alone in all the
universe now shines more brightly than the sun.'' In brief,
according to the recapitulated formula of Filofei: "Two
Romes have fallen, but a third stands; and a fourth there
shall not be." Time and again he tried zealously to impress
these religious and political axioms upon Grand Prince Vasily.

The second volume of *Outlines of Russian Culture*
recounts the national and religious consequences that
resulted from the theories just mentioned. In the end these
theories led to the complete nationalization of the Russian
Church. But here another aspect of these doctrines is more
important, that is, the national and political sanction that
emanated from them. In this respect it is necessary to
investigate one more important step that these theories
(which were linked to the South) made upon Russian soil
to accommodate themselves to local authority.

According to this new theory, the Muscovite "Tsar
and Autocrat" was the direct continuer of the work of
Tsar Constantine. But the leap from the "old" Constantine to the "new" was too great. Hence, this succession
was presented as a *logical* result of events in the Orthodox
world. Yet for the sake of complete persuasiveness and
clarity it had to be presented as an *historical* fact that had
occurred in time and space, at a precise moment and in a
definite place. The same had to be done to coordinate the
South Slavic formula for Muscovite political pretensions
with native Muscovite pretensions. In his practical politics
the Muscovite prince seemed an heir of his own "ancestors;"
he had obtained the inheritance of "the Grand Prince of
Kiev" as his own "patrimony and grants from his forefathers."
He was of course prepared to play the role also of heir of
Tsar Constantine, but only with the condition that this
ideological inheritance did not obscure the other, which
was incomparably more practical and accessible. Thus the
Balkan ideology had to be reconciled with Muscovite
politics.

With the help of the newcomers from the Christian
East the problem was resolved brilliantly. So that the
Byzantine inheritance should not obscure the Kievan, it
was best to invest a Kievan "ancestor" with this Byzantine
inheritance and to link him directly to the great names of
antiquity. Were not the two Vladimirs the two Kievan
ancestors who were rooted in the national memory more
firmly than all other princes? Who could more adequately
play the role of heir to Byzantine authority than he who
bore the Greek sobriquet, Monomakh, a name that recalled
this prince's blood ties with Byzantium?[5]

Concocting fantastic genealogies to justify national
political pretensions was nothing new for Slavic writers. As
early as the eleventh and twelfth centuries they had portrayed
the Bulgarian Asens as being from "a distinguished Roman
family," while in the fourteenth century they had related the
Serbian Nemanja family[6] to Constantine the Great and even
Caesar Augustus. Ivan III undoubtedly also felt the need
for more magnificent historical connections of this sort,
something that might do more to equate his eminence with
that of the Emperor than simple reference to his Kievan
ancestors could do. Now he made an official attempt to
link himself to Tsargrad and Rome, but not directly, as the
husband of Sophia Paleologos could do easily, but through
his own "ancestors." He still resolved not to speak of kinship
and the formal transmission of authority. But here is what
his ambassadors told the German Emperor in 1489, several
months after Poppel's embassy: "It is known in all lands,
and we trust that it is also known to you, that our Sovereign
is a great Sovereign who was born from the very beginning
of his own ancestors *and that his ancestors* from bygone
years were in friendship and amity with *the former Roman
Tsars*, who returned Rome to the Pope and themselves
reigned in Byzantium."

At the beginning of the sixteenth century the legend
finally assumed concrete forms. There appeared in Moscow

the complete tale of "the Princes of Vladimir,"[7] which satisfied
the previously mentioned needs of the Muscovite government.
According to this tale, "Augustus Caesar" established "Prus,
his kinsman," on the banks of the Vistula River. A fourth
generation descendant of this Prus, Rurik by name, was invited
from the "Prussian land" to Rus by the "men of Novgorod."
The fourth descendant of Rurik was St. Vladimir, and the
fourth descendant of St. Vladimir was Vladimir Monomakh.
This sobriquet then provides the author the occasion to relate
an entire history, for which purpose the entire tale had been
invented.

On the advice of "his princes and boyars and nobles,"
Vladimir undertook a triumphant campaign "against Thrace."
The pious Constantine Monomachus,[8] who was then Tsar and
was occupied with a struggle against "the Persians and the
Latins," sent to him ambassadors with gifts: "a little cornelian
box that the Roman Caesar Augustus had enjoyed," a necklace,
"that is to say, sacred mantles" from his own shoulders, a
golden chain and "many other royal gifts." The ambassadors
entreated "the good prince who was beloved by God" to
accept "these precious gifts as his royal lot for the glory and
honor and coronation" of his "free and autocratic kingdom."
This lot has been prepared for him and for "his kindred and
his generation from the beginning of time," "so that God's
churches should be tranquil and all Orthodoxy remain at
peace under the rule" of the Byzantine "Tsardom" and "free
and autocratic Great Russia," so that the Muscovite prince
"who is crowned with this royal crown" will be called "a Tsar
crowned by God." "From that time and henceforth," the
author of the tale adds in the conclusion that he found
necessary, "the grand princes of Vladimir, when they were
elevated to the grand princes of Russia, have been crowned
with that royal crown that was sent by the Greek Tsar
Constantine Monomachus."

Whoever may have been the author of the "Tale of the
Princes of Vladimir," whether Pakhomy the Serb, as a recent

scholar has asserted, or some other writer of the same milieu, there is no doubt that the "Tale" was the logical outcome of all the ideas disseminated throughout Rus by the South Slavic clergy beginning in the second half of the fifteenth century. Yet despite the great importance of these ideas for the government, despite the semi-official character of this literary creation, the Muscovite government did not immediately resolve to use these strategems openly or to confer official sanction upon these novel political views.

It should be added that during the era of Ivan III these views were still being elaborated. Along with this influx from the South Slavic world came another that was directly contradictory and sharply oppositionist. The fermentation of semi-official and oppositionist elements continued from the late fifteenth century to the mid-sixteenth century. Only then did official acts of the government finally clarify and consolidate the inventory of ideas that had made their way into the national consciousness. Before dwelling upon this final outcome, however, we must become acquainted with the oppositionist ideas that entered Rus and investigate their fate in this new situation.

V

HERESY, MYSTICISM AND COUNTER IDEOLOGY

We have seen how life itself prepared the soil for *nationalistic* ideologies in the Muscovite state of the fifteenth century, and how political ideas imported to Russia from the lands of the South Slavs quickly began to develop on this soil. But the fate of *oppositional* ideologies in Rus during the fifteenth and

sixteenth centuries was completely contrary. Partly introduced
from an alien source, these ideologies found the soil poorly prepared for them and, after a brief struggle, had to quit the field
of battle before their victorious enemy. The history of this
struggle and this victory must now be retraced.

The order in which oppositional ideologies evolved in Rus
during the fifteenth and sixteenth centuries had become typical.
Initially they displayed primarily a religious coloring. Then a
political element was linked to the religious. Finally a social
element emerged, although this was independent of both the
foregoing. Following this sequence, our story shall also begin
with the most abstract form of opposition, in order to conclude
with the most natural.

As is well known, religious freethinking in Rus first
appeared in the most cultured districts — Pskov, Novgorod
and Kiev — as early as the fourteenth and fifteenth centuries.
Researchers assiduously have sought the sources of this free-
thinking in the West and the South, in the sects of Medieval
Germany and in the Bogomil Heresy.[1] The second *a priori*
explanation seems more likely, for even the most cultured
areas of Rus then were unprepared for the influence of the
West, especially in the realm of religious thought. The first
Russian heresy had to come from the Orthodox East.

This consideration leads us back to the very source
from which we have just deduced the political ideologies of
Muscovite Rus: the Balkan Peninsula. Amid the religious
ferment in the Balkans of the fourteenth century were two
orientations important to our study, for they were closely
connected with Russian movements of the same time. I
refer to the *heretical* orientation and the *Orthodox-mystical*
orientation. At this time Bogomilism revived as a true heresy
and, it seems, somehow became linked to the rationalistic
doctrine then widespread among the Balkan Jews, who were
then rather numerous.

According to the fragmentary information of the sources,
the Bulgarians and the fourteenth-century Jewish heretics from

Solun[2] were accused of precisely the charges leveled against the Russian "Judaizers,"[3] namely, refusal to accept the birth of the Savior from the Virgin Mary, rejection of icons, disrespect toward the saints and their relics and repudiation of the resurrection of the dead. Naturally, Jews cannot be expected to accept all these dogmas. But they apparently propagated their views actively among the Orthodox. In view of the Jews' extensive commercial operations, it is hardly surprising that this propaganda spread from a large Jewish trading center, as was Solun, to the Crimea and to Kaffa and its local Karaites.[4] From Kaffa these doctrines began to traverse borders overland as well and, passing through Kiev, reached the Lithuanian Jews. Meanwhile, according to the direct testimony of our sources, the "Jewish heresy" arrived in Novgorod from Kiev.

With respect to true Bogomilism, the route by which it succeeded in reaching Rus cannot be established with equal certainty. It is most natural to surmise that this heresy made its appearance in the company of another religious movement that originated in the Balkan Peninsula, the mystical movement of the so-called "Hesychasts," with whom the heretical movement undoubtedly maintained ties even after Bogomil and "Hesychast" doctrines were transmitted to Rus. The intermediary that hastened this transmission could have been the Orthodox center, Mt. Athos.[5]

Throughout the entire fourteenth and fifteenth centuries Mt. Athos was truly the heart where all interests that stimulated contemporary Orthodox thinking found their fullest expression. The concerns of Mt. Athos were not generally as elementary as might be judged from the state of Russian religiosity at that time. The Orthodox East had advanced far beyond Orthodox Rus. In general the East found excitement from the same things that stimulated European religious thinking of the period. It fluctuated between nominalism and realism or, to be more precise, between scholasticism and mysticism. When the founders of theoretical Slavophilism

strove to represent scholasticism strictly as a peculiarity of
western thought and to make mysticism a privilege of the
East, they undeniably erred. Both modes of religious thought
existed in the East as well as in the West, although the West
expressed both of them more vividly.

But the error of the Slavophiles is easily explained by
the fact that mysticism (especially during the period discussed
here) truly was practiced on a very broad scale in the Orthodox
East. In the fourteenth century its preacher and theorist was
Gregory Sinaites, whose teaching was developed by his fellow
countryman, the Greek from Asia Minor, Gregory Palamas.[6]
The successors of both men were Bulgarians: Theodosius and
Euthymius of Trnovo. The teachings of all these religious
thinkers drew very near the boundary beyond which mysticism
ceases to agree with the staid teachings of Christianity and
becomes pantheism. All of them begin, like the Slavophiles,
by denying "syllogism" and science, or "external wisdom," as
a means of knowing truth. They hold that truth can be
attained only be becoming absorbed in one's own soul. They
contrast theoretical "knowledge" with moral and religious
"activity." But to attain the highest level of "love of wisdom"
possible for man they prefer inner, mystical "contemplation"
(*theoria*) to "activity" (*praxis*). And to reach the full depth
of "contemplation" they recommend a number of practical
methods common to mystics. Through these methods a state
of ecstasy is achieved and is physically expressed by certain
gestures of the body and a peculiar feeling of peace (*hesychia*,
hence "Hesychasts"), rapture, and finally, at the highest level,
"the light of Mt. Tabor."[7] This final state, the feeling of light,
marks the state of complete union with the Godhead. To
reconcile this notion of direct union with God to conventional
Christianity, Gregory Palamas had to concoct a unique distinction between the "essence" of God and His "manifestation"
(*energiia*). The former is unfathomable; but man can merge
with the latter.

On Mt. Athos, where Gregory Sinaites, the founder of

this doctrine, lived for a long time, the theory of the "Hesychasts" was very much in favor. At this precise moment in
the fourteenth century the Bogomils made their impact upon
Mt. Athos. The two teachings shared more than a few points
of agreement in the positive features of their doctrine as well
as in their negative attitude toward everything in traditional
religion that hindered their "inner" understanding of the
faith. Their disregard for ritual and externals, their preference
for the living spirit over the dead word, their hostility toward
any bureaucratic notion of pastoral duty — all these similar-
ities linked them so closely in the eyes of their enemies that
accusations that the Balkan "Hesychasts" and those from Mt.
Athos were part of the Messalian Heresy (that is, Bogomilism)
became commonplace. Because the critical aspect of the
teaching of the "Hesychasts" was easier to understand, this
aspect had to predominate when these views migrated to Rus.

At that time Russia possessed one man who could most
fully appreciate the theory of Gregory Sinaites. He was Nil
Sorsky,[8] who had become familiar with the teachings of the
"Hesychasts" on Mt. Athos itself, whence he introduced these
doctrines to Russia. Above all else Gregory had demanded of
his followers strict seclusion. But the ordinary "communal"
monastery did not satisfy this demand. For this reason Nil
introduced a new regime of life for his own disciples, the hermitages. In a remote region beyond the Volga, around the
Kirillov Monastery,[9] quite a few of these "hermitages" were
founded and were inhabited by "hermits,"[10] followers of
Nil, who came to be called the "Trans-Volga Elders." This
style of life enabled them to translate into reality their "non-
possessing" ideal of monastic life and to criticize monks and
monasteries that owned property — lands, villages and peasants. Their goal in all this was obvious: to quit the world.
But, wholly unexpectedly, their beliefs were found to have
political significance and, contrary to their primary concern,
they were forced to play a prominent role in a secular political struggle.

In Russia religious controversies generally assumed a nature that very quickly involved both Church and state. Whenever religious doubt arose in the Orthodox East, usually it was resolved by an ecclesiastical council. The teachings of the "Hesychasts," for example, had been judged and accepted by three such councils during the fourteenth century. In Rus things were different. "This thing, heresy, which is unheard of among us," took the native ecclesiastical authorities completely by surprise and evoked not theoretical discussion but administrative persecution. "Our people are simple," wrote the bishop of Novgorod, Gennadius.[11] "They cannot talk in the manner of books. Thus it is better not to engage in debates about the faith. A council is needed only that heretics be judged, burned and hanged." But the sovereign did not immediately approve the summary justice recommended by the archbishop.

The reason for this was, first of all, that the heretics of Novgorod were supported in Moscow by an influential faction that apparently shared their convictions. These were all men of some learning. One of them even converted to the new teachings the daughter-in-law of the grand prince, Elena, whose party, the Patrikeev clan, was then powerful at court. The metropolitan of Moscow, Geronty, therefore kept silent, "either through lack of comprehension, or through negligence, or out of fear of the ruler." His successor, Zosima, evidently was supported by Elena's party and shared its views.

But there was yet another reason why Ivan III did not hasten to deal with the heretics. In 1478 he had taken from the clergy and monasteries of Novgorod fully half their lands. The heretics were preaching precisely this sort of "nonpossession." In this regard, the theories of the Russian "Hesychasts" (that is, of Nil Sorsky and his disciples, the hermits) were even more opportune for Ivan. They were not such inveterate heretics as the "Judaizers" of Novgorod and hence would not scandalize the Orthodox flock by their views as much as did the "spiteful wolf," Metropolitan Zosima.[12] For this reason

the grand prince continued to hold Nil "in great honor" after
Ivan deposed the patent heretic, Zosima. This "great honor"
was very much part of Ivan's politics, that is, the subordination of the clergy to the authority of the state.

During the consecration of Zosima's successor, Ivan addressed the new metropolitan, Simon, in a sermon that contained something of an inauguration. At this point Muscovite
authority claimed a right that earlier had belonged only to the
Byzantine Emperor, the right to confirm the nomination of
the metropolitan. Four years later, in 1500, Ivan once again
removed from the jurisdiction of that same Simon certain
lands of the clergy of Novgorod and imposed on the remainder
a heavy tax on tilled acreage. Finally, three years later, an
ecclesiastical council was summoned in 1503 under an innocent
pretext, that of deciding the status of widowed priests. After
the most prominent defenders of the interests of the clergy had
departed from this council, Nil and his disciples, the "Hermits
of Beloozero," to everyone's surprise, "began to say that monasteries should possess no villages and that monks ought to
live in the wilderness and be fed through their own manual
labor." In effect, this would mean the complete secularization
of monastic properties in Russia. Obviously these Russian
"Hesychasts," who were more moderate in their religious views
than their counterparts on Mt. Athos, did not yet feel constrained to resort to compromises in applying their program;
for the grand prince was personally behind them.

Those who defended the past took alarm. Quickly they
summoned Joseph, the abbot of Volokolamsk and leader
of the traditional Orthodox party, who had departed the
council before its conclusion. Without waiting for his arrival,
the metropolitan sent his secretary to the grand prince with
a letter. Then high ecclesiastical officials from Moscow and
Joseph himself appeared and read to Ivan a rejoinder in which
Joseph proved through numerous quotations (some of which,
in truth, were not cited honestly), if not the moral justice
and legality of monastic patrimonial properties, then at least

their historical sanction from antiquity and their legal propriety. The grand prince had to retreat before these precedents from ancient times, for it would have been awkward to force matters to a radical conclusion. With this his alliance with the "non-possessors" lost all practical importance for the grand prince.

Ivan's conscience then awakened. He summoned Joseph of Volokolamsk and confessed that in truth he had supported the heretics but promised to investigate the matter and finally eradicate the heresy. Still, the "non-possessors" did not yield immediately; this is evident from further wavering and procrastination on Ivan's part. Obviously disturbed by new arguments advanced by the "non-possessors," Ivan again summoned Joseph and asked him: "How is it written? Is it not a sin to execute heretics?" Gennadius' associate naturally found no difficulty in selecting examples and quotations to dispel the apprehensions of the grand prince. Yet the matter dragged on. Following his futile reminders to Ivan, Joseph had to engage in literary polemics with the "non-possessors" to refute doubts that still troubled the grand prince. The abbot of Volokolamsk steadfastly maintained that "it is all the same to kill a sinner with your hands or with your prayers." The "non-possessors" ironically suggested that Joseph try to work against the heretics one of the miracles attributed to him and recalled that the Gospel forbids one to judge his fellow man.

This first publicistic controversy in Rus ended to the detriment of those who had sought innovation. A council summoned in 1505 complied with all the wishes of the defenders of the old ways. The heresy in Novgorod was obliterated by brutal persecutions. So ended the history of religious free-thinking during the era of Ivan III.

In the reign of Vasily III the struggle between new ideologies and old customs assumed new forms. Taught by experience, the non-possessors no longer defended their earlier positions. Nil's successor, Vassian, seems less profound and less erudite than Nil, but more practical and down to earth.

He was not one to sacrifice reality for the sake of theory or
to defend radical measures merely because they were logical.
Daily life demanded compromise, and Vassian advocated
compromise. No longer did he deny the right of monasteries
to own lands but only attempted to argue that they should
not own people. For its part, Joseph's party also made a concession: it acknowledged the right of secular authorities to
control the use of monastic properties. But now the controversy ranged far beyond its previous boundaries. A political
element was added to the purely religious theories of the
opposition; and this finally determined the fate of Russian
religious freethinking.

As long as the non-possessors were accused, more or
less justly, of having secret sympathies and dealings with the
heretics of Novgorod, state authorities could look at this
through their fingers and continue to use the services of this
party for their own aims. But once the political reliability
of the religious opposition became suspect, it became another
matter. It was natural that the opponents of the non-possessors
should seize the first opportunity to impart a political tint to
the controversy. A suitable opportunity arose during the first
years of the reign of Vasily III, in 1507-1509.

Joseph's monastery was located in the appanage of
Volokolamsk. The local appanage prince, Feodor Borisovich,
tempted by the example of Ivan III, began to claim a portion
of the properties and coffers of the monasteries in his district.
To escape his extortions, Joseph transferred his monastery to
the direct supervision of the grand prince. At that time there
was no one in Rus to whom complaints could be made concerning Joseph's action. But the prince of Volok found an
indirect way to revenge himself upon Joseph. It happened
that Joseph's immediate superior was the prelate of Novgorod,
whose blessing was required before Joseph could transfer his
monastery to another diocese. Joseph obviously had done
what he had done because he was well acquainted with the
prelate of Novgorod, Serapion, and could count on his support.

"Under the influence of the Novgorodians who were well disposed toward the prince, or perhaps out of his own sense of justice," one researcher has observed, "Serapion could not sympathize with the idea that an appanage prince should be deprived of the right to manage a rich monastery, which was taken over by the 'state ruler,' who was also prepared to help himself at any time to his first cousin's last appanage." Joseph, on the other hand, had no reason to fear opposition to what he had already done, either from the prince or from the bishop. "Do not trouble yourself about this (the bishop's blessing)," Vasily himself had said to a messenger from Joseph. "But tell Joseph that it was *not he* who departed from the archdiocese of Novgorod; rather, *I myself* took the monastery from under the power of the appanage prince. When our national adversity is over,[13] I myself shall send word of this to the archbishop."

For two years Serapion awaited this "word" from the prince without receiving it. Then, incited by the prince of Volok, he took a decisive step; he expelled Joseph from the priesthood and from the sacraments. "You have deviated from the spiritual and have gone over to the earthly," he wrote in his statement of excommunication to Joseph.

"The matter took a political turn," the same researcher has observed. "Serapion's statement was discussed on its own merits. In this statement he had called Prince Feodor spiritual, but the great autocrat had been characterized as earthly. Herein could be seen the spirit and the sedition of Novgorod." The metropolitan of Moscow hastened to absolve Joseph of the excommunication imposed upon him by the prelate of Novgorod. Serapion was called to Moscow, where he was stripped of his priesthood and was interned in the St. Andronik Monastery. Yet this did not force him to abandon his defense of what he considered right. From his internment he wrote a letter to the metropolitan in which he did not ask to be invested with his former powers but developed his arguments, which the council that had censured him had refused to consider, and declared for all to hear that "in truth he feared neither the Prince nor the masses of people . . . , for it is written: Speak the truth before Tsars, and do not be ashamed."

Such conduct by the deposed bishop then caused a sensation even in Moscow. Serapion found supporters both in Novgorod and in the capital, especially among the boyars. Joseph's adherents were disturbed and one after another turned to him with the request that he make peace with Serapion. Joseph replied with a number of letters to friends in which he not only refused to admit any guilt but, on the contrary, sharply attacked his adversary and sought theoretical justification for his action. In these letters Joseph frankly emphasized the political character of the entire episode and thereby defined the position taken by his own party during the initial stages of this political struggle.

"Sacred laws command the Church and the monasteries," Joseph wrote, "that they should approach the Orthodox Tsars and Princes with their injustices." "Church people have always and everywhere appealed from lesser Tsars and Princes to the greater." Following their example, Joseph also has petitioned him "who is Sovereign not only of Prince Feodor, but of Archbishop Serapion and of us all, the common Sovereign of the entire Russian land." The sovereign's "Lord God has set him in his place and has established him upon his royal throne, giving him justice and mercy and entrusting him with the Church and monasteries and power over all Orthodox states and the entire Russian land. If I had petitioned another sovereign, then I would have acted improperly." Serapion, on the other hand, "disgustingly had opposed the divine laws." "Cast judgment on the head of Serapion who, rather than submit humbly at the council to the Orthodox Sovereign and Autocrat of all Rus and even the most reverend Metropolitan, began to argue with the Sovereign and those who are consecrated. But divine laws command that we respect the Tsar and not quarrel with him. The saints of old did not dare to do so,

nor did the four Patriarchs or the Roman Pope when he
attended an ecumenical council. Whenever the Tsar was
angry with anyone, they entreated the Tsar with meekness,
humility and tears." Therefore only "foolish people, who
are like beasts," can offer Serapion encouragement. "So
you, Sovereign, stand firm and do not shame the faces of
those who are good." In short, Joseph developed the well-
known theory of "studied slyness."

This viewpoint was indeed a complete contrast to the
theory of the non-possessors, which Serapion had implemented. The non-possessors desired that the Church stand
above the sovereign and, for this reason, especially should
be independent of him. The source of dependence is property. Renunciation of property would ensure therefore the
independence of pastors from the secular powers that be.
Only under such circumstances would ecclesiastics find it
possible to turn to the authorities, not with their "injuries,"
but with their "grievances" concerning the falsehoods of
the world. A simple comparison between this point of view
and the notions Joseph defended suffices to determine
which side the Muscovite authority had to support.

Joseph did not offer the authorities religious sanctions
over the clergy *without cost*. He took advantage of his
altercation with the prince of Volok to demonstrate through
the testimony of the Scriptures the consequences that arose
when authorities meddled in inviolable monastic properties.
From formidable examples drawn from the past he concluded
that "not only does God abrogate the power of those who
steal from the Church and take monastic property. He also
deprives them of their souls, with terrible and cruel torments."
In other words, Joseph demanded that the Muscovite government leave monastic property in peace.

At this point the authorities were prepared to compromise. Even Ivan III was constrained to forego complete
secularization of Church property. Vasily III restricted himself to simple control, against which even the abbot of

Volokolamsk, as we have seen, had no objection. Against this background the final union between the "Josephites" and the authorities was realized.

The non-possessors and their lofty aspirations were relegated to the oppositionist camp. The membership of this camp is apparent from the story just told of Serapion. It comprised what survived of the spirit of Novgorod after the severe measures taken by Ivan III. Of course, merely sorry fragments of that spirit still persisted. Later there could also be found in the oppositionist camp the remnants, somewhat better preserved though scarcely more vital, of the power of the appanage princes with whom Ivan III had settled once and for all.

VI

BOYAR OPPOSITION

It would be erroneous to conclude that all opposition in fifteenth-century Russia was composed exclusively of the appanage princes, these ruins from the past. There was yet another element, one that did not simply disclaim the new order being established in Moscow but strove in its own way to adapt to this order, while demanding in it place for itself. The *boyars* — and not only those who had lived long in Moscow, but also those who recently had moved to the capital from their princely appanage thrones — lived not in the past but in the present and wished to become established therein as favorably as possible.

From their ancestors of the fourteenth century the Muscovite princes of the fifteenth and sixteenth centuries

had received the injunction to "listen to the boyars." The
strength of the boyars meanwhile had grown both in quality
and in quantity. The range of their activity also had broad-
ened extraordinarily. The boyar council was now a necessary
institution of state; the small group of people who participated in this council as part of their service obligation during
the appanage period had been transformed into an undivided
social class that regarded the role of advising the sovereign its
exclusive political right.

At first these pretensions encountered no rebuff from
the prince of Moscow; on the contrary, these ambitions
served as an additional resource for the formation of a new
system of government. The boyars became one of the most
useful of the prince's adornments. When, for example, Ivan
III received from Lithuania a document from "the council of
all the Princes and Pani"[1] of the Lithuanian principality, it
bore an address that Ivan found unusual: "To our brothers
and friends, the Princes and Pani of the council of Grand
Prince Ivan Vasilievich." Ivan did not wish to be humiliated
by these [foreign] teachers of governmental law. Therefore
the Russian princes and boyars were commanded to affix
their signatures to the reply, which was composed in the
chancery of the prince. So that the Lithuanian "council of
Pani" should not have cause a second time to plead ignorance of the Muscovite boyars "and the places where each sits,
and who sits beside him in the council of the Sovereign,"
this document recorded both the names and imaginary titles
of the Muscovite advisers to the prince: "From Prince
Vasily Danilovich, the voevoda[2] of Moscow, and from Prince
Danil Vasilievich, voevoda of Great Novgorod, and from
Yakov Zakharievich, voevoda of Kolomna," and so forth.

Thus the very desire to imitate neighbors elevated the
Muscovite boyar council to the level of a regularly organized
institution of state. For precisely the same purpose Ivan
also copied his own title from Polish-Lithuanian charters.
But apart from this showiness, Ivan undoubtedly valued his

duma[3] as a truly useful institution when faced with complicated problems of government. Not without reason did Ivan secure for himself a good remembrance even among such adherents of the ruling class as Prince Kurbsky.[4] In Kurbsky's opinion, Ivan III "expanded his borders so far, drove off the Great Khan of the Horde and destroyed his yurt,"[5] because "he received much advice from wise senates and greatly loved counsel, undertaking nothing without much profound advice."

Yet even during Ivan's day there crept into these relations a dissonance that rapidly developed into basic opposition. The level of consciousness of this opposition grew in keeping with the development of the national, political ideologies already noted. The more fully the theory of autocratic power evolved, the more incompatible it seemed with the attitudes of those former princes who "greatly loved counsel." But *on the other side*, among the boyars, the course of events prompted *completely new ideologies*, which progressively intensified the opposition just noted.

The power of the two factions, of course, was far from equal. When one side took the offensive, the other could only defend itself. This is why the weaker and vanquished side, the boyars, became accustomed to perceiving its ideology mainly as defensive and the ideology of its enemies, the sovereigns, as aggressive. The boyars were ready to accuse the Muscovite grand prince of "abandoning custom" and to portray themselves as the defenders of the past. But it would be a grievous error to take them at their word. In reality neither side was the more attuned to the past, although both tried to demonstrate that historical tradition was on their side.

The right of "counsel" in government affairs was the primary desire of the boyar class. The boyars believed that they had long had this right; the entire matter was now one of preserving this prerogative under the new order. "The land became troubled," as they saw it, only after the arrival in Moscow of "the Tsarevna from Tsargrad" (Sophia). Only then did it become ever more difficult and riskier "to speak out against the

ruler." All this was absolutely true. But it was also true that
formerly such pronouncements "against" the ruler were far
fewer, nor were they considered a *right*, much less the *exclusive* right of a definite social class. Only when discussion of
state matters, which had grown complex in nature and greater
in number, had become the permanent occupation of a specific
group did each refusal, each attempt to bypass this body or to
circumvent its prerogatives begin to be felt as a wrong by the
members of this united group. In the eyes of the boyars it was
wrong when the "adviser" of the prince became (not only in
position but in title as well) a certain Shigona Podzhogin,[6] and
when the prince pondered his thoughts with "his own bed
chamberlains." It became offensive that the prince "trusts his
scribes very much, yet chooses them not from the gentry, nor
from among the nobles, but rather from the sons of priests or
from the simple folk at large, and thereby creates hatred among
his magnates." This "offense" on the one hand and this "hatred"
on the other were something novel, results of the fact that it
was now necessary to divide that which previously had not been
divided.

At stake was not simply a struggle between an old, obsolete order and a new, emerging order, but between two political
ideals, vastly unequal in strength, struggling for their future
realization. These ideals were first formulated with full consciousness and articulation during the third generation after the
beginning of the struggle, in the famous correspondence between
Ivan the Terrible and Kurbsky.

"Why is he called Sovereign and *Autocrat*, if not because
he himself creates?" Ivan IV asked his adversary. Foreign
sovereigns "do not rule their kingdoms; they rule as their subjects wish them to." Such kingdoms have perished because
"there the Tsars listened to bishops and councils. If subjects
do not obey the Tsar, civil strife never ceases in that country."
In truth "the land is ruled not by judges and voevody, nor by
the five provinces,[7] nor by strategists, but by the grace of God,
the prayers of all the saints, the blessings of our parents and in
the end by us, its sovereigns."

Kurbsky, the first Russian emigrant, who had voluntarily left an "ungrateful, barbaric" homeland "unworthy of its learned men," which yet remained "dear," in no way desired to accept such a point of view. He would not acknowledge that "God had committed" his ancestors to "labor for the forebears of the Grand Prince." To Kurbsky the princely clan was merely "the blood-sucking family of olden times," which based its power upon the law of strength. Kurbsky's political ideal was the dual power of the Tsar and the "chosen council."[8] The Tsar should be the head and his advisers the members of the same body. Incidentally, this prince-publicist did not limit himself to the desire that members of his own class should participate in this "council." He went further. "The Tsar should seek good and useful advice not only from his advisers but also from all the people of the nation." Though indignant, as we have seen, with the "scribes" elevated by the ruler to an unseemly height, he had nothing against such members of the "chosen council" as Adashev,[9] a nobleman of lower rank.

Such was the character of the political opposition with which the religious opposition of the sixteenth century formed an ideological union. We last saw this religious opposition in the third stage of its existence when, ceasing to be heretical (as with the Judaizers) or radical (as with Nil Sorsky), it prepared to compromise with the demands of reality in the person of Vassian. Vassian's very affinity to practical life, however, brought him face to face with contemporary political reality. As the consecrated representative of a disgraced princely family (the Patrikeevs),[10] he felt the full weight of the political regime being established in Moscow. Without becoming enamored of any political theory, without trying to create any political ideal, he nevertheless could not help but reflect the political evil of the day, all the more so since he had been close to Tsar Vasily and had enjoyed great influence at court.

"Grievance" to the "ruler" was the sole form in which

this prince-monk and his confederates could protest the contemporary events troubling their conscience. It was natural that the progressive clergy should adhere just as firmly to the right to express grievance as the boyars clung to the analogous right of "counsel." The very similarity of their situations drew together the non-possessors and the discontented boyars, especially since there was nothing to alienate them. The rivals of the boyars in landowning were not the non-possessors but their opponents, the defenders of the patrimonial estates of monasteries. The non-possessors desired no more than moral influence upon the secular authorities.

The following example illustrates the political opposition mounted by the non-possessors during the reign of Vasily III and the consequences it produced. In 1523 a prince of North Russia was compromised by letters to Lithuania and was imprisoned in Moscow, despite a written guarantee of safety given him by the grand prince and the metropolitan (who was a Josephite).[11] The metropolitan, who "took his oath upon the icon of the Holy Virgin, the saints and his own soul," was the first to rejoice at the capture of this "relentless enemy" of the grand prince. But the non-possessors looked differently upon the actions of the prince and the metropolitan. They not only censured this act in conversations among themselves (which later served as one of the grounds for the incrimination of Maxim the Greek[12]), but one of them, the Abbot Porphyry of the Trinity Monastery, "a man of simple habits and trained in the *desert*,"[13] resolved to "beseech" the sovereign "to free his brother from bondage." For this he was banished from his monastery and was subjected to torture. That same year Maxim's turn also came, for he was an idealist who, at the commands of the Gospels, had subscribed to the entire religious program of the non-possessors, to their struggle against the monasteries' greed for money and to their "grievances." Further, he had listened to their complaints about the dismal reality of political life, which was not only wild and alien but even difficult for a student of Savonarola to understand. Maxim

was condemned more for the opinions of his party than for
his own views. Six years later Vassian followed him into imprisonment.

Thus the third generation of oppositionists departed
the stage without having benefitted the cause they had espoused. But the seeds they had cast did not immediately
decay. On the contrary, during the fourth generation
(even if such pinnacles of political thought as Kurbsky and
Ivan the Terrible are omitted) the oppositionist theory was
elaborated further, as was the theory of autocracy. Ivan
the Terrible's perspective was promoted and defended by
new arguments, as in Ivashka Peresvetov's[14] famous pamphlet,
"The Tale of Peter, the Voevoda of Wallachia." In answer,
an unknown author developed Kurbsky's political theory in
the so-called "Dialogues of the Miracle-Workers of Varlaam,
Sergei and German."[15]

The Tsar must be "awesome and self-governing and
wise without questioning (that is, without another's counsels);" only then "will God subdue his enemies beneath his
feet, and he will possess many kingdoms." Here is the basic
proposition that underlies all of Ivashka Peresvetov's subsequent discourses. The first consequence of this position is
that counsel with "friends," his nobles, can only weaken the
strength of the Tsar's initiative. Like Ivan IV himself, Peresvetov was inclined to deduce all governmental calamities
from a single cause: "The nobles by their magic have captured the heart of the Tsar and have taught him to follow
their will in all things." For this reason "justice has been
diminished in the Muscovite state."

Having enriched themselves and grown lazy, the
nobles "depart upon their merrymaking, gaily on horse-
back, in crowds." But while they are going to battle, they
trample down the people and lose their army, thanks to
their cowardice. Keeping towns and rural districts for their
own feeding,[16] the nobles grow rich on the tears and blood
of the peasants. They hurl corpses into the homes of the

rich and into villages, to bring ruin upon those who will be
accused by an unjust court. They become partners of tax
collectors, allowing them "to gather money without mercy,
to torture peasants and to take ten rubles for the Tsar, but
a hundred for themselves." In short, by doing the will of
the nobles, the Tsar "thereby launched an unnecessary war
against his own kingdom." No one had access to the Tsar,
for these same nobles "beat off from him those who came
with petitions."

These shady intermediaries between the Tsar and his
people had to be abolished. To act apart from them and
to turn to the people from the Place of the Brow,[17] this
was Ivan IV's way; and this was also the theory of his defender. Thus inspired, the exposure of injustices caused by
administrators under Peresvetov's pen became a broad picture of the social ills from which Rus suffered and from
which it could be liberated only through the direct interference of Tsarist power. We shall soon return to this feature of the "Tale."

Peresvetov's monarchist theory did not remain unanswered and elicited from Muscovite constitutionalists of
the sixteenth century a sharp rejoinder. This rejoinder,
which contained its own party program, was expressed in
the curious pamphlet written by some admirer of Vassian.
This piece is interesting primarily because its author combined the theory of the non-possessors with the theory of
the oppositionist boyars. Through the mouths of the holy
"monks," Sergei and German, the creator of this "tale"
(the title of which derives from their names) developed an
entire theory, which most originally merges and intermingles
the ideas of the religious opposition and those of the political
opposition — the notions of Nil Sorsky and Kurbsky.

"Many have wrongly thought (this expression is taken
from Peresvetov's conclusion, to be discussed below) that
God created man with a will of his own. But had he created
man to be absolute, then God would not have given us Tsars

and other authorities and would not have separated one kingdom from another." The author agreed that the state was
created "for the temperance of the world, in order to save
our souls." But for this it is not enough that sovereigns be
"awesome." They cannot do everything through their own
efforts. They must seek counsel, especially the counsel of
people from the rural communities. In reality, the sovereigns
of more recent times have proved to be "simple." They have
controlled the village community *not with their friends, the
princes and boyars,* but with the "unburied dead," the monks.
The monks, who have renounced the world, own rural districts
and peasants, judge laymen and release them on bail. The
monks make their living by the tears of the peasants, collecting
for their own use all royal revenue from their districts, as
though they were the temporal stewards of the Tsar. By acquiring rich mansions they have ruined their souls. Hence, the
villagers show little respect for those clergymen who wander
through the villages because they have lost their offices.

To elevate ecclesiastical authority it is first of all necessary to gather all property revenue into the treasury and to
allot the clergy an annual fixed salary. Secondly, all homeless
ecclesiastics must be subordinated to monasteries. Then the
village community will become secure and the kingdom strengthened through the fasts and prayers of monks, their unceasing
tears and standing at prayer. They will see to it that every man,
high and low alike, confesses each year, lest the Tsar have to
answer before God for the souls of his subjects. And the Tsar
himself will rule with his officials: "He will take counsel with
his advisers on all matters." In a supplement that some scholars
(groundlessly, it seems) attribute to another author, this pam-
phleteer makes a highly original connection between his two
conceptions: saving souls through annual confession and the
Tsar's administration of all affairs of state with the advice of
men from the communes. The Tsar should strengthen and en-
large his realm not through his personal bravery but through
the wisdom of his glorious army. The clergy must bless the

Tsar "at a concerted ecumenical council." And the Tsar must
"with joy but without arrogant pride, with humble Christian
wisdom, annually raise up from all his towns and from the districts of those towns people of every walk of life and keep
them continually by his side, daily informing himself well from
these people concerning the yearly fast and the confession of
the entire community and everything that happens in the community." In this manner "the Tsar always will have knowledge
of all the affairs of his autocracy," and he will be able to preserve from sin all his officials, his voevody and his authorities:
from graft and promised favors and all the countless sins that
accompany power, in a word, from all injustice.[18] These "people who must fast all year" will also ensure that all others make
their confession each year, so that both souls and bodies will
be preserved.

More was involved here than merely the development of
theory. There is every reason to believe that these citations
from the "Dialogues of the Miracle-Workers of Varlaam" were
simply a belated literary expression of views that the Russian
opposition of the sixteenth century had earlier attempted to
attain in practice.

It might be expected that such an attempt would be
made during the period of boyar rule following the death of
Vasily III. But Elena's regency[19] did not prove an especially
favorable moment to implement an oppositionist ideology. On
the other hand, circumstances were more propitious at the end
of that troubled decade, when Ivan IV came to the throne.
This was the era that Kurbsky paints in such rosy colors and of
which Ivan the Terrible speaks with such anger as the time
when Sylvester[20] and Adashev "did and approved everything
according to their wishes and the desires of their advisers,"
when they left Ivan only his name and his honor, but conferred upon themselves all the power of the sovereign.

At this time the idea of an ecclesiastical and national
"ecumenical council" became a reality. The series of questions
that the Tsar submitted to this first council in many instances

closely resembled the ideal of the author of the "Dialogues
of Varlaam." First and foremost the "Dialogues" discussed
the question of monastery properties, although there immediately arose a second point, no less vital to the state, concerning the form of remuneration for military service, that
is, the question of service lands. It is known that the question
of the morals and inner discipline of the clergy was linked to
the problem of monastery property. On this last point the
author of the "Dialogues" is not far removed from Kurbsky's
sweeping views. Also, Russia was greatly confused by new
vogues from the West and the East, new dress and hair styles,
new decorations for rooms, new manners of singing in church
and in painting icons, that is, new directions in ecclesiastical
painting and music. The author of the "Dialogues" called all
these matters to the attention of the government and its advisers.

Other sources emphasize that the series of issues just
outlined as being at the basis of the "Dialogues of Varlaam"
greatly interested the "chosen council" of Ivan IV on the
eve of the convocation of the council. First of all, the young
reformers who comprised the "chosen council" remembered
their old leaders. Maxim's voice from prison and the voice
of another non-possessor, Artemy,[21] who had been exiled to
Solovki[22] shortly thereafter, were the first to ring out in ap-
peal to Syvlester and Adashev. Both, of course, had championed reform. Artemy had even alluded to the possibility of
a radical resolution of the problem of monastic property in
the spirit of Nil Sorsky.

But the time for radical resolutions had passed or, to put
it better, had never come. Metropolitan Macarius,[23] despite
his gentleness and habit of doing things agreeably, here remained
faithful to the precepts of his *alma mater*, the Monastery of
Volokolamsk. Macarius delivered a forceful opinion against
raising the radical question at the impending council by following the custom of citing the words of another (Metropolitan
Simon, at the council of 1503). He was supported also by

several who did not favor the enterprises of the younger party.
Hence, even before the council convened, it was clear that
the matter of monastic property would end in half-measures.
The membership of the ecclesiastical council that assembled
in Moscow in 1551 (the so-called *Stoglav*[24]) did not arouse
any special hopes. Of its nine members only one (Vassian) was
known for progressive views. For this reason history has
adorned his biography with the most imposing details, such as
that his arm was paralyzed, his head turned backwards, and
so on. Three (in addition to Macarius) were "Josephites," open
enemies of reform.

 We cannot dwell on the work of the council here. Suffice
it to say that in regard to the patrimonial rights of monasteries its work was limited to several measures dealing with state
control of monastic courts and financial administration of
monasteries. In addition, a new kind of head dress ("the skull-
caps of the godless Mohammed") was subjected to brutal
suppression, as were new styles of icons and the practice of
shaving the beard. The governmental measures adopted in the
interests of the service class were much more important.
Rewarding generals for service and protecting the way of life
of officers became the true watchword of the day, something
that Kurbsky had advocated, but Ivan the Terrible had attacked.

 To provide for this officers class, the first Russian *zemskie sobory*[25] were summoned. It has been shown that the first
sobory were neither gatherings of true popular representatives
nor full expressions of popular opinion, as the author of the
"Dialogues of Varlaam" would have wished. The government
convoked its own servitors who held important positions,
then demanded not so much their vote as their expert opinion.
Thus it happens that as soon as this seemingly interesting
institution first appears, the historian of Russian social movements can learn nothing from it. It ends up merely as one
more ecclesiastical council of the oppositionist movement that
had lasted a full half-century, a fact that kept its results to a
minimum. For the same reason no new movement could origi-
nate from these *sobory*.

VII

ROOTS OF POPULAR OPPOSITION

By resolutely protecting the interests of a single class (and, it should be noted, not the class then in power and whose influence would soon prove so precarious, the boyars, but the class to which the future belonged, the middle service class), the Muscovite government thereby nurtured new opposition. This opposition was the least ideological but the most dangerous, even when manifesting itself passively. We refer to social opposition, the opposition of peasants and bondmen.

The first signs of social opposition appeared prior to the *sobory*, in advance of any conscious and systematic class legislation. To be sure, this social note had been sounded amid all the polemics hurled against monastic ownership of lands and people and had generated moral, religious and political motivation. It was particularly strong among the hermits, as well as among those enemies of monastic property who were not slave owners and who attacked the monks not as dangerous competitors in the business of service landholding, but on principle. Maxim the Greek, who was most moderate in his political views and most abstract in his moral judgments, in this instance uttered his sharpest and most irrevocable censure. "Where is it written," he asked, "that (monks please God) by loaning money contrary to the provisions of the law or by extorting from beggars interest upon interest? Yet we permit ourselves to do this to the poor peasants, who work and suffer without respite in our villages and at all our services, hindering their lofty

development and ruining them when they cannot discharge
their debt . . . . You torture a man and plunder his wretched
homestead; you drive him and his wife and children from
your villages with empty hands or enslave him in eternal slavery,
just as the ancient torturer, Pharoah, enslaved the sons of
the Israelites. If, when he is exhausted by the weight of the
labors constantly imposed upon him, he wishes to move
to some other place, we do not allow him to do so without
paying the established quitrent, forgetting his countless
labors and sufferings and the sweat spilled for the services we
have needed during the many years he has spent in our village. What can be more loathsome than this, my brother? What
can be more inhuman?"

Those who were closer to contemporary Russian life than
Maxim could not but feel that the brunt of these accusations
fell not only upon monastic landowning and slave owning. Any
small landholder or great boyar did the same things in his
villages. It seems, therefore, simple blindness or carelessness
when the author of the "Dialogues of Varlaam" echoes Vassian
and Maxim in his own recriminations against "monks who
make their living from the tears of members of the peasant community," yet carefully shields secular landholding from the
same accusations. In any event, his position was extremely in-
consistent. Not only monks made their living from the tears
of the peasant community; not only monastic oppressions can
explain the passive popular protest to which Maxim alluded
in the words reproduced above. The author of the "Dialogues"
characterized this protest still more clearly in a prophecy:
"There will be emptiness and no one to oppress. In the villages
the peasant dwellings and the people themselves will begin
to diminish; and the land will become more vast, while the people will be fewer. And the people who remain in that vast
land will have nowhere to live." If the single radical conclusion
reached by the author of the "Dialogues of Varlaam" could
advocate seizure by the state of all monastic lands and payment
of an annual salary to the monasteries, it was completely

consistent to propose the *extension of this measure to service
landholding as well.*

This is how the above-mentioned pamphlet by Ivashka
Peresvetov also posed the question of rewarding the service
class. The social aspect of this work merits attention. First
and foremost, Peresvetov sharply underscored the calamities
experienced by the lower classes that gave rise to the domi-
nance of the boyars. The nobles who have seized the realm,
he insists, "do not restrain the strong for the sake of the poor
and the helpless. A weak man cannot either dwell in the town
or stray from it even a verst. Many, therefore, surrender themselves to noble households to save themselves from misfor-
tunes. But God has not commanded us to enslave one another.
God *created man sovereign* and commanded him to be his
own master, and not a slave. We ought not to register a man
for labor and record him forever."

Peresvetov held that there is but one conclusion. "So powerful a sovereign as the Russian Tsar must take the revenue from
his entire kingdom directly into his treasury and from this treasury must pay his military and civil officials an annual salary,
whereupon he will be able to live with his people and his warriors
year after year. The Tsar must reward his military servitors,
bind them close to himself, hear their complaints and thereby
comfort their hearts. Then as few as 20,000 warriors would be
more powerful than 100,000 under the existing order. Then
the nobles will cease "their unrighteous gathering of riches,
their taking precedence according to family and their seeking
of preference,[1] which weakens the Tsar's army." By having
his "army" in his own hands, the Tsar will be able to "seduce
his nobles in every imaginable way and to *play with his boyars,
like infants.* The nobles will begin to fear him and will not
dare come hear him with any sort of evil cunning."

But the democratism of this defender of Ivan's policies
goes no further in criticizing the social conditions of contemporary Russian life. Peresvetov sides with the "poor and
helpless" only in a very conditional sense. He does not side

with the peasants against their masters, but does side with the "army" against the "nobles." He finds no objection to counseling the government to deal directly with the peasants, thereby circumventing their lords, but this only to the extent that the interests of those lords, insofar as they coincide with the interests of the state, are preserved. Should it seem that direct relations with the peasants under such conditions are impossible to establish, the government should not hesitate for a moment to subordinate the "army" to the "sovereign individual, the ruler himself," "for everlasting labor."

It must be remembered that these notions emerged only with the passage of time and in the course of events. Whatever the virtues of this program of monarchy and democracy, its main and recurrent interest lies in its negative aspect, that is, the struggle against the nobles and the social calamities that would befall anyone whom these nobles opposed. Boris Godunov went so far as to propagate this program graphically by ordering that the Palace of Facets be painted with pictures in which the Tsar was depicted as "sorrowing" because of the "sedition of the nobles," then turning them over to a just judge to mete out retribution. The same pictures portray a widow demanding justice against a noble who is wronging her, and so forth. This was a pictorial response to a painting done earlier (in 1552) in the neighboring Golden Chamber, which recalls both the "chosen council" and even Sylvester, the highest source of royal wisdom, who here is likened to Barlaam in the famous fable of Barlaam and Josephat. Even art participated in the polemics between the two parties of the sixteenth century.

Thus the social question evolved during the sixteenth century in two directions: first (among the non-possessors and their supporters) in a religious and moralistic direction; then (at the hands of such oppositionist pamphleteers as Peresvetov) in a political direction. Both orientations were unable to benefit from the social question, because each used it only as a means of struggle against its opponent. Social opposition in the true sense was concentrated in social "strata" that could

formulate no social "question." When this opposition emerged
in its own right, its appearance took the form not only of
theory but also of deeds.

One of these deeds had already been noted by the author
of the "Dialogues of Varlaam," when he predicted that "the
people will begin to diminish and the land will become more
vast." In reality, as the dream of Muscovite publicists was realized and the boundaries of the state were expanded, especially
to the east and south, the number of people fleeing Muscovite
ways to the free borderlands began to grow ever greater. In
the final quarter of the century these flights became massive
and began to threaten almost complete depopulation of the
center of the old state. The national economy of the center
was faced with complete havoc, and state authorities, who at
first had regarded the refugees as a colonizing force useful for
its own purposes, finally felt constrained to identify their
interests with those of the landlords, the service people. Under
such circumstances talk necessarily arose of implementing
the idea of democratic monarchy, as contemplated by Peresvetov,
concerning the defense of the "sovereign individual" against
encroachments upon its freedom by the ruling classes. The
government limited itself to another task, also not easy, inasmuch
as the *oprichnina*[2] and serfdom were required for its realization:
the task of protecting the army against designs upon it by the
nobles and against their rivalry in the realm of landholding. This,
too, was essentially the main idea of Ivashka Peresvetov's pamphlet.

The social opposition, of course, was not eradicated
merely because the government ceased to think of it. Elements
of this opposition continued to accumulate on the frontier.
At first opportunity they were to remind the government of
their presence. This opportunity presented itself during the
Time of Troubles.

It is interesting that the banner of this first active social
protest was the "true Tsar Dmitry," and not the boyar Tsar,
Vasily Shuisky. The lawful successor of Ivan the Terrible

evidently impressed the Russian people as their true patron
and protector *against* the boyars, who dreamed of the possibility of reviving the traditions of Kurbsky's "chosen council."
Ideas of democratic monarchy, we see, were consciously pre-
ferred by the Russian people to the constitutional ideas of
the boyars, in the name of which Vasily Shuisky gave his "guarantee" that he would put no one to death without the judgment of the boyars and would not resort to arbitrary confiscation of the property of his subjects. Thus Peresvetov's
theories collided with the theories of the "Dialogues of Varlaam" in real life and proved to be more popular.

These theories contained two nuances that did not quite
harmonize with each other on paper; still less could they
be combined in real life. They defended against the boyars
the *army* primarily, but also the lowest class of those enslaved (not only by the boyars but by that very army): the
peasants and bondmen. Both these elements rose "against
the boyars because of the murder of Dmitry and the unwar-
ranted election of Vasily Shuisky." In the land of Riazan
the "army," that is, the service people, rose in rebellion. In
the land of Seversk refugee peasants and bondmen rose up,
those who had been dismissed by boyars in time of famine,
or who had been driven from homes confiscated by boyars,
or who had simply fled of their own will.

Soon it became clear that both elements could not act
in unison and be allies, inasmuch as the goals of their
struggle and their tactics were totally different. Runaway
bondmen had no interest in merely changing dynasties.
Their leaders painted for them the perspective of a complete
social revolution. In their proclamations they "commanded
the bondmen of boyars to kill the boyars and promised
them the wives, patrimonies and service lands of these boyars;
they ordered nameless vagrants to kill merchants and all
commercial people and to seize their property. Calling these
brigands to rally behind them, they promised them the status
of boyars and voevody and courtiers and state secretaries."

To be sure, during the first successes of this movement the
northern rebels began in the name of the true Tsar Dmitry "to
destroy the homes of boyars, to seize their property and take
their wives; they killed boyars and voevody in various ways,
throwing them from towers, hanging them by their heels and
crucifying them on the walls of towns." In short, they reproduced all those scenes that are so well known from the history
of social movements of the eighteenth century. The gentry of
Riazan quickly abandoned such dangerous allies and returned
to union with the lawful authorities, which then did not hesitate to execute the enemies of the social order. For two whole
years the government of Vasily Shuisky hanged and drowned
these "brigands;" the entire province of Seversk was proclaimed
a theatre of war and was given over to the plunder of foreigners,
such as the Cheremis[3] and Tatars.

At last the government felt the need for legislative intervention in the realm of social relations, yet in no way
provided for the interests of the "sovereign" individual. In
1607, immediately following the uprising, we encounter
a number of measures, the general aim of which was to subordinate the bondmen of boyars to governmental supervision and to halt the exodus of peasants to the frontier. So
ended this first manifestation of social protest against the
new Muscovite order.

The sources of opposition to this order were now fully
exhausted. The order had proved stronger than the ideologies
advanced against it and even stronger than the social interests
that were at variance with it. If, despite all this, these ideologies
were able to assert themselves earlier with sufficient clarity,
it was because they were bound to do so for the reason that,
first of all, this order had not yet become fully established and,
secondly, the Tsar offered his protection to some of these
ideologies, while other were protected by the only other strong
social element of that time (except for Tsarist power), the
boyars. In the seventeenth century both these considerations
no longer had any effect. The order was finally established,

and the boyars were deprived by Tsarist policies of all political significance. Small wonder that the seventeenth century saw nothing resembling that clash of heterogeneous principles evident throughout the sixteenth century. New political ideologies emerged, to be sure, in due course. But they developed, so to speak, outside the established social order.

VIII

TRIUMPH OF THE NATIONALIST PROGRAM

Such were the elements from which the social self-consciousness of Muscovite Russia was moulded. The content of the nationalistic and oppositionist ideologies of the fifteenth and sixteenth centuries has been surveyed above. Which of these was to triumph was completely predetermined by impersonal circumstances in the political and social life of Muscovite Russia. The first sections of *Outlines of Russian Culture* attempted to depict these circumstances, which now presumably are well known. These circumstances caused the foreign policy of the Muscovite government to raise the banner of nationalist ideologies that were both governmental and religious, while domestic policy began to adhere to the political program advocated by Ivashka Peresvetov.

A nationalistic foreign policy arose at the end of the fifteenth century and was finally completed and formulated in the second half of the sixteenth century. The social and political program of domestic policy was delayed somewhat. The government still fought for such a program during the second half of the sixteenth century and realized its decisive victory only in the seventeenth century, after the ordeals of the

Time of Troubles. The triumph of both programs must be studied in somewhat more detail.

The Cathedral of the Assumption in Moscow still preserves a vivid testimonial to the moment when the nationalistic ideology of Muscovite state power officially triumphed. The Cathedral contains a Tsar's throne with a canopy in the form of the hipped roof so common to Muscovite churches of the time, with shutters on three of its sides. On each shutter four scenes are depicted in finely carved workmanship. A carved text explains the meaning of each scene, which recounts the legend we have discussed earlier, of how the Greek Emperor of Constantinople, Monomachus, sent to Vladimir Monomakh the royal regalia. In 1547 Ivan the Terrible was solemnly crowned Tsar and officially adopted the title of Tsar. In 1552 he ascended that royal throne, an action that conferred official sanction upon the legend of the continuation of Byzantine authority.[1] In 1561 Ivan won formal recognition of this legend from the Patriarch of Constantinople. To do so it had been necessary to scrape away bits of a Greek charter containing some things that were not quite what the Tsar desired from the Patriarch. Be that as it may, the deed was done, and the Muscovite government could appear ceremonially before foreign powers with its new pretensions.

These pretensions, it is true, did not receive immediate recognition. In 1581 Bathory[2] advised Ivan "not to repeat the fables of your braggards" about Prus and Augustus Caesar being your "relatives." But Ivan did not leave this unanswered and triumphantly refuted the doubts of his rival with one simple consideration: "If Prus has never lived, let King Stefan explain to us the origin of the Prussian land!" Then it was Ivan's turn to express doubts. Having such eminent lineage, could Ivan, without suffering loss of his dignity, communicate on equal footing with one not "of sovereign descent, but from the rank of knights," as was Bathory?[3] Ivan had an even meaner appreciation of the Swedish king, that he was directly from the "common people." When the Muscovite Tsar received

a letter from the "Sovereign of the Indian Land," he confronted
a great difficulty, whether to call him a brother in his reply.
Ivan finally decided "not to write him of brotherhood," for it
was uncertain "whether he is a sovereign or a simple village
policeman." In the language of Muscovite political theory the
meaning was clear: "Is he an absolute sovereign or a limited
sovereign?" Moscow had extremely low regard for limited mon-
archs. "We were of the opinion," Ivan wrote to the English
Queen, Elizabeth, "that you were sovereign in your state and
ruled it yourself. But now we see that the people rule, and
not only the people but peasants and merchants . . . . You merely have the status of a girl and behave like a common girl."
Ivan treated the "miserable" power of the Polish king just as
contemptuously. "You are an appointed sovereign, not a
patrimonial sovereign," Muscovite boyars wrote to Sigismund
Augustus. "Because your Pani wanted you, they gave you
the kingdom as your salary. If your own will is not free, how
can you rule your kingdom freely?"

The achievements of this nationalistic self-exultation cul-
minated in 1589 with the proclamation of the complete independence of the Russian Church from the Greek Church and
the appointment of a Russian Patriarch. Once again official
acts profited from a legend that had become popular much earlier. The theory of Moscow as Third Rome, of the superiority
of Russian Orthodoxy, of religious (as well as political) succession
from Byzantium — all this was transferred from the literary
sources of the beginning of the century to the state document
that sanctioned the institution of the Patriarchate at the end
of the century. Yet even in this instance reality could not satisfy
proud national pretensions. The Muscovite Patriarch was
placed last in the series of ecumenical Patriarchs, despite efforts
by Muscovite diplomats to secure for him at least third place,
if not first place.[4] But the diplomats were forced to yield this
point, inasmuch as the agreement to create the Patriarchate had
been extracted from the Greeks almost by force.

There is every reason to believe that the triumph of

nationalistic theories was not restricted to government circles.
During the sixteenth century these theories had begun to
come to the attention of the populace as well. Whenever an
idea spreads among the people, invariably it gains a foot-
hold in the national memory in the form of a national legend,
assisted by metre and rhyme. Legends recorded during the
sixteenth century, as well as official statements, also found their
way to the public at large, who perceived these legends not
with their eyes but with their ears. The people naturally con-
fuse names, events and dates while transmitting this living
tradition orally and from memory. But the general significance
of these events is well remembered.

Thus the Russian people incorporated into its recollection
the nationalistic legend concerning the Prince of Moscow's
acquisition of the Tsarist regalia. Emulating the written sources,
the national telling of this legend had its hero sent from
Tsargrad to Babylon in order to procure regalia for the *Byzantine* emperors. But then the national imagination developed
a style of its own. When the messenger, Theodore Barma (whose
name obviously suggests the *barmy* of the Tsars[5] returned
to Byzantium, he found the kingdom and the faith in ruins and
delivered the regalia directly to the sole ecumenical Tsar,
Ivan Vasilievich. Barma met the Tsar just at the moment of
his triumph over the Moslems and when Ivan was finally
assuming the title of Tsar. "Here in Tsargrad there was great
bloodshed. The Orthodox faith had fallen and the Orthodox Tsar was no more. So Theodore Barma went to our neighbor, Russia, came to the town of Kazan and entered the
palaces of the Prince, the palaces of the heroic Prince . . . .
Here the purple[6] and the crown from the city of Babylon was
placed upon the head of the dread Orthodox Tsar, Ivan
Vasilievich, who had pulled down the kingdom of the scoun-
drel, the pagan Prince of Kazan."

What is still more interesting, the national memory not
only recalled the moment when Muscovite state power
was exalted but also preserved the notion of a connection

between nationalistic foreign and domestic policies. In
national epics the new power of the state was presented
either as an instrument for struggle against domestic enemies or as a result of victory over them. Monarchy was depicted as part of a democratic program of action, as has been
reproduced on the walls of the Palace of Facets in Moscow:

> When the red sun rose
> Then our dread Tsar ascended the throne,
> The dread Tsar Ivan Vasilievich.
> He gave a splendid and honorable banquet;
> Everyone at this banquet slaked his thirst,
> And everyone at this banquet bragged.
> But the dread Tsar Ivan Vasilievich said:
> "Let no one but me brag of being Tsar.
> I have received my royal power from Tsargrad.
> I have clad myself in the royal purple;
> I have taken in my hands the royal scepter;
> *And I shall drive treason from stone-walled Moscow.*"

Or, in another version:

> From Pskov I have driven treason.
> From stone-walled Moscow I have driven treason.
> In passing I took the Kingdom of Kazan,
> And bent Tsar Simeon to the ground.
> From the Tsar I took the royal purple
> And brought that purple to stone-walled Moscow.
> I blessed the purple in stone-walled Moscow.
> I placed that purple upon myself.
> After this I became the dread Tsar.

Here, too, a fresh remembrance was preserved of how the
living, not the legendary, Tsar Ivan Vasilievich really did
"brag" before his people from the Place of the Brow, shifting
all blame for disorders in the state to the boyars and
promising to redress all things; or how a decade and a half
later this same Ivan the Terrible publicly stated his dis-
favor of the higher strata of society and his favor toward the
lowest, then requested extraordinary powers from the

latter to deal with his and their enemies, in order to "drive
out treason."[7]

IX

SOCIAL CLASSES AND TSARIST AUTOCRACY

We have seen that Ivan's domestic policy and that of his supporters really was not at all as democratic as would appear
at first glance. The "red sun" that was "rising" over Russia
quickly was discovered to be the bloody glow of a social
conflagration. In keeping with Peresvetov's theory, the
"army" (that is, ordinary military servitors) increasingly
became the sole source of concern on the part of the government. The army came to be considered an element necessary to the existence and independence of the government,
as well as a support against claims by the "nobles." The
middle service class [*dvoriane*] were endowed with lands.
Their burden of taxation eased. They even were consulted
on governmental affairs. On the other hand, Ivan "stood for
himself" against the upper social stratum, in the interests
of self-preservation. He "ruined" this stratum "throughout
the entire state" and proceeded so successfully that by the
end of the century the boyar class was merely a pitiful
remnant of what it had been at the start of the century. As
far as the lowest social stratum was concerned, it simply
lay beyond the reach of the government. The government
was concerned with this stratum only when necessary for
the good of the "army;" and, of course, the government regarded this stratum just as did the "army."

The top and bottom of Russian society were necessarily

dissatisfied with this situation. At the top there still barely
glimmered the spark of the old and almost completely
extinguished political opposition. At the bottom inflam-
mable material rapidly accumulated, threatening to blaze
forth in the form of social protest. In the final analysis
both elements were unable to coexist with the weaker middle strata of society, the service class of the Muscovite
state. Yet political circumstances were such that in a brief
span of time these extreme elements were to dominate
the middle.

The outward cause of this totally fortuitous development was the demise of the dynasty. The internal cause,
which was in no way accidental, was the ease with which
various social groups could mobilize their forces to take
advantage of evolving conditions. The boyars, who had recently lost their ruling power, were closest to the power that
had just fallen from its habitual wielders. The boyars were
the first to attempt to exploit the Time of Troubles for their
own advantage. But they were too poorly disciplined and
too much interested in using their own representatives to resolve the dynastic problem in favor of specific candidates
to profit as a class from the struggle now beginning. Moreover, the boyar class was too shattered by the policies of
Ivan the Terrible. The surviving fragments of this group were
too divided by considerations of lineage to form any sort
of real power. The sole weapon of the boyars was court intrigue, a weapon that was highly effective in more peaceful
times but absolutely useless before the difficult circumstances
in which the state now found itself, thanks to the intervention of foreign enemies and other groups during the Time of
Troubles.

The schemings of the boyars more than once had confused the street crowd of Moscow, which was quite disor-
ganized and was powerful only when assembled in a mass.
Small wonder, then, that this crowd, when organized into a
permanent military organization as were the Cossacks and

the runaway peasants and bondmen that allied with them,
found it highly possible to gain control of a given situation
for more or less extended periods of time. The weakness of
this group lay in its ability to win a victory one day and its
inability to exploit that victory the next day. The Cossacks
were suited to play the role of soldier of fortune; yet they
found no employer in this capacity, nor were they suited for
an independent role in politics. When the Cossacks allied
with runaway peasants and bondmen, they estranged themselves
from all propertied classes and forced these classes to adopt
measures of self-defense against them. Rightly or wrongly, the
contemporary bourgeoisie was convinced that throughout
the Time of Troubles the Cossacks retained their "basic evil
intention," discernible as early as the uprising of Bolotnikov,[1]
that they wished "to kill the *better people*, the boyars and
the middle service class and people of all ranks, as well as state
and district officials, plunder their properties and rule according to their thieving, Cossack custom."

Even the most indecisive were prompted to action by the
spectre of social revolution. The middle stratum of society
found it especially difficult to organize for any sort of action.
Only extreme necessity could force it to rise; only very
slowly could it put its affairs in order and enter the arena.
But once this group began to play an active role, it necessarily
took as its objective the restoration of the former order under which it had lived better than other social groups. Essentially, then, this element was conservative. Its victory over
the last outbreaks of political opposition (the boyars) and the
first outbursts of social protest (the Cossacks) was to clear
the way for the triumph of the national program of domestic
policy.

Very often it is said, in keeping with the rhetorical expressions of chronicle writers, that the Muscovite state
was saved by the "lowest people." If by the "lowest people"
is meant the prosperous merchants, as Muscovite servitors
were accustomed to call them in their genealogical calculations,

Kuz'ma Minin[2] must certainly fall into this category. But it
must be remembered that such a "commercial man" as
Minin also had his antipode in Fedka Andronov,[3] who supported Wladyslaw and Sigismund.[4] One peculiarity of
this period was that people of this stratum generally were
able to gain a voice in social matters. Nor is there any
question that such people were also needed by any government
as taxpayers and tax-gatherers, and that a strong government
found them indispensable for their commercial enterprises and
trading operations. *After* the service people, they were really
the most necessary element in society.

It is hardly surprising that aspirants to power tried to win
to their side both the merchants and the servitors. Both
groups were divided among various aspirants before time could
decide which of them would prove to be "true" and which
"false." "You should without any doubt assemble with all your
people and come to us in Moscow," Tsar Vasily Shuisky tried
to persuade those who had fallen away from his province, "and
perform your service and zealous work. We shall grant you
our great salary. To you, the service landholders and *deti boiarskie,*[5] we shall grant much money, as well as service estates;
we shall order you to be settled on estates and given our salary.
And you, townspeople and district inhabitants [*uezdnye*],[6]
we shall reward with privileges for many years. We shall command that you be allowed to trade free from customs and
shall bestow our *tarkhan* charters[7] upon you for everything.
Above and beyond this we shall grant you a great salary,
which you cannot even imagine." This charter demonstrates
with extraordinary clarity the elements upon which the
government could depend and how it could compensate them
for their "service."

There was indeed a moment when the "townspeople and
rural inhabitants" *alone, without* the help of the servitors
(the "service landholders and the *deti boiarskie*") stood Tsar
Vasily in good stead. This occurred when the established
middle service class left the "boyar class" of the Tsar to go

home or to Tushino,[8] while the Muscovite Far North, organized by Skopin[9] from Novgorod, supported him. In the North there were no service people at all; there were merely townspeople in the towns and state peasants in the districts. When these "muzhiks"[10] arrived in central Russia from their northern homelands, the populace became greatly "confused." These truly were the "lowest people" of the state, and in central Muscovy it was customary to regard them as nothing more than Cossacks and their runaway companions. But the civil militia hastened to dispell these fears. "You are confused," they wrote to the inhabitants of the town of Romanov, "because men of lower strata supposedly put to death those of the middle service class and the *deti boiarskie* and destroy their homes. But *here*, masters, *the men of lower strata honor the middle service class and the deti boiarskie,* and there is no infamy attached to them."

In reality these men from the maritime regions had nothing in common with the Cossacks of South Russia. They were simply recruits who had been furnished by their village communes on order of district authorities and were supported by local state taxes that in part were designated for this purpose. By sending these recruits to the assistance of the government, the townspeople were fulfilling a customary obligation to the state, though not as readily as in times past, for they now risked finding themselves in service to a government that was not lawful. While the peasant militia was being recruited in the North, the people of Ustiug, for example, were writing to the inhabitants of Sol'vychegodsk: "Please, think firmly of peace and do not hasten to swear your oath. Do not try to guess how things will turn out . . . . If we hear that God will send His righteous wrath against the Russian land, there will be time before it reaches us. We shall still have time to render our homage." This calculation proved to be completely correct. By the end of the Time of Troubles the state-controlled rural districts of the Russian North and their leaders from the towns naturally exhibited even less inclination to "hasten."

For this reason the *real* "lowest people" of the Russian land played an insignificant role in the outcome of the Time of Troubles.

The main role undoubtedly was played by the service class. Had this class succeeded in becoming organized in good time and had found an early candidate to ensure its interests sufficiently, the Time of Troubles would have reached a much earlier conclusion. Long before the service class formed its own representation during the Time of Troubles, its social strength was already obvious. This group came to be depended upon as a most reliable element and governmental action was undertaken on its behalf. In addition to this class, it is true, the name of the townspeople arose whenever the voice of the *entire* land was mentioned. But everyone understood that the actual representative "of the entire land" was the service class, the military men. Whenever towns communicated with each other, their official representatives corresponded among themselves; and these were, with the exception of the state-controlled North, their "great members of the middle service class." Whenever there was talk of a "unanimous council of the land," everyone knew that the qualitative and quantitative majority at such a council would be formed by the service class. In theory, of course, the council was to be one of "all ranks of the Muscovite state." But among *"all* these ranks" every possible service group, even the most petty, was recorded in the most exact manner, while the tax-paying populace of the districts merely was mentioned obscurely at the end of the customary formula for the sake of stylistic completeness. In fact, usually they were omitted.

This does not mean that the events of the Time of Troubles left no room for more impassioned elements and more idealistic motivations. Undoubtedly both could be found and even exerted considerable influence upon the disposition of individual features of events. But the general meaning of these events was precisely as we have said, and those who played roles in their unfolding sensed this very clearly. Vasily Shuisky was overthrown

as a consequence of a national meeting held outside the Arbat-
sky Gates of Moscow. The meeting formulated its business
in proper expressions, as follows: "The middle service class and
the *deti boiarskie* of all towns, the *gosti*,[11] the commercial
people and all people, as well as the *streltsy*, the Cossacks, the
townspeople and people of all ranks of the entire Muscovite
state, having talked among themselves, . . . all have petitioned
the Sovereign that the Sovereign give up the state." If indeed the "middle service class" and others had not backed the
motley Muscovite throng, Vasily's overthrow would have
been unthinkable. In the same manner Kuz'ma Minin could
have been right when he placed on the lips of Saint Sergei
the words: "The elders will not embark upon such an undertaking, if it is not begun by the youngsters." Still, it would
be strange to explain the successes of Pozharsky's[12] militia at
Moscow by the enthusiasms that Minin had inspired in the
youths from Nizhni Novgorod.

The closer the idea of a national council "of the entire
land" came to realization, the more distinctly unfolded
the program of action with which the new government was
to be charged by its constituency. During the period
when correspondence had been conducted between the
towns, it had become absolutely clear to the social group
that had just come onstage that the interests of the other
two camps, the boyars and the Cossacks, must be cast aside.
Even before the town militias[13] gathered in Yaroslavl,
they had given each other written commitments to remain
in concert in their opposition to both the boyars and the
Cossacks. Once they had pushed aside these groups that had
been deeply involved in the Time of Troubles, the service
detachments from the towns simply ignored all other "ranks."
To their mind, the term "the entire army" was fully synonymous with the expression, "the entire land."

How this attitude was reflected in the social considerations
of the service class is evident from the terms it dictated to
those it elected: to Wladyslaw in the pact of August 17, 1610;

to the triumvirate of Trubetskoi, Liapunov and Zarutsky[14] in
the "verdict" of June 30, 1611; probably also to Pozharsky;
and, finally, to Michael Feodorovich himself. The first two sets
of terms are well known. The last two we can surmise.

With every new change of power the program of the military men developed with increasing fullness and consistency.
The basic principle of this program was that the voice of the
service people from the towns was the voice of "the entire land"
and that it should be heard on all the most important state
problems. This principle had been recognized much earlier by
the spokesmen of authority. We do not refer only to Boris
Godunov, who was the first ruler to practice a definite policy
of protecting the service class. Even the boyars' elected
representative, Vasily Shuisky, tried to gain the support of
the entire service class as a means of opposing the intrigue of
the boyars and the "sedition" of the people. Instead of an
oath to the boyars, he tried to take a universal oath, "to
the entire land," and thereby greatly irritated those who had
elected him. Later, when a mutinous mob appeared in the
royal palace, Tsar Vasily told them to their faces, in the words
of the chronicle: "If you wish to kill me, I am ready for
death. But if you desire to topple me from the throne, you
cannot possibly do so without the great boyars and the
middle service class and *without a council of the entire Russian land."* When, a year later, military servitors came to
depose Vasily, they did so in the name of all ranks of the Muscovite state. Having dethroned the Tsar, the victors swore,
and forced the Russian land and the provisional government
they established under Prince Mstislavsky to swear, to
"choose a Sovereign for the Muscovite state from among the
boyars and all the people of the entire *land* . . . , in agreement with the towns."

The army men immediately demonstrated that by the
terms "all the people" and "the entire land" they primarily
meant themselves. Not waiting until a complete council
could be assembled and without further dealings with "the

land," they launched preliminary negotiations with a candidate
of their choice, Prince Wladyslaw. To his provisional government the middle service class attached a single condition: "to
judge us all with fair judgment." Having reached a permanent
agreement with this foreign candidate, they sought to develop
this condition into a complete program to serve as the subject
of a formal contract. The rough draft of this contract was
composed at Smolensk by deputies of the middle service class
who had come there from the camp at Tushino. Its final
form was ratified near Moscow and was signed by Ziolkowski[15]
and the boyar regime. This circumstance has led researchers
to accord special (and in our opinion exaggerated) attention to
the few changes that were made during its final drafting. It
has been assumed that these alterations predominantly illustrate
the *boyar* motivations in the contract. In reality, the influence
of the middle service class was the key element in this wording.
Not without reason did the middle service class so jealously
follow the negotiations of the provisional government with Ziolkowski and later appeared before Ziolkowski in large crowds
of about five hundred men.

If those points of the contract are excluded that deal with
the simple reconstruction of the old governmental order, as
well as those describing the relations between the Russian land
and the foreign candidate, his fellow countrymen and his
government (points that flowed from the peculiar conditions
of the moment and the personality of the candidate), the
remainder of the contract with Wladyslaw was most concerned
with the preservation of the interests of the service class and,
as a component part of that class, the boyars. The representatives of "the entire land" first and foremost sought to up-
hold the *status quo* in relation to the service class: "monetary
compensation, quitrents and service lands and patrimonial
estates, and what was held before these events." Then they
squabbled about commutation of their taxes and dictated to
Wladyslaw a measure that later was adopted by Tsar Michael
in the interests of the service class. They demanded that

"someone be sent" to districts desolated by the war "to inventory and investigate how many were killed and to command that the *living* receive revenue according to this inventory and investigation, and to award patrimonies and service estates as privileges to those who have been neglected, after talking with the boyars." Finally, they used this opportunity to bind to themselves the working force and projected another measure adopted by the new dynasty. "Among themselves the peasants will not have the right to leave; the boyars, the middle service class and all ranks will keep the bound people in accord with previous custom, by title deeds."

X

**SERVICE PEOPLE, AUTOCRACY AND THE
TIME OF TROUBLES**

So it was that all the essential interests of the service people were protected. It remained merely to ensure that in the future, during normal times, their voice would be heard during every governmental reform that concerned them. It was not that the servitors failed to gain this earlier; rather, they had considered it unnecessary in the agreement with Wladyslaw. Only with respect to "just judgment" had they seized the occasion to impose a more definite and compulsory resolution upon the government. "Judgment will be accorded in keeping with past custom and according to the *sudebnik*.[1] If there is reason to replace anything in order to strengthen the courts, this must be agreed to by the Sovereign and his council of boyars and *the entire land*, that everything might be just." This is the sole instance in the contract where the necessity of convoking a assembly of the land [*zemskii sobor*] is envisaged. Moreover, this was also the sole case in which the new dynasty still deemed it necessary to resort to a council even after the idea of appealing to "the entire land" had long gone out of fashion. Apparently just judgment was too vital a need to be ignored; and any refusal to grant it would be felt with too many misgivings by "all the ranks" of the Muscovite state.

All other current business the service class calmly left to the government after stipulating only that "members of the council" [*dumnye liudi*] be consulted on the more important matters. Here, too, was introduced a regulation implemented during Shuisky's election: "Not to find guilty and not to judge through a court *any of the boyars*, nor to execute anyone, nor to deprive anyone of his honor, nor to imprison anyone, nor to deprive anyone of service land or patrimonies or homesteads," nor to extend guilt to the relatives of a criminal.[2] Here was the formal revocation of the law formally recognized by the entire Russian land at the insistence of Ivan the Terrible, when Ivan undertook to "drive treason from stone-walled Moscow." Another important regulation was inserted, one that had, according to information provided by a foreign visitor, figured in Shuisky's pact with the boyars: "State revenues shall be collected as in the past, and nothing shall be increased over and above the former customs *without the say of the boyars*." In both these instances the service class, though surrendering an important category of affairs to the jurisdiction of the boyar *duma*, simply followed its favorite idea of returning to "old custom." Never did it think that the boyars would be strengthened thereby.

The single measure in the contract directly favoring the boyars was engendered by the fact that the Tsar was a foreigner. He was obliged "not to constrain or demean the honor of the princely and boyar families of Muscovy in favor of foreign newcomers to our country." But this obligation stemmed from the principle stated in the pact that generally barred Poles and Lithuanians

"from participation in the administration of justice and from
serving as governors in the towns; nor could Poles and
Lithuanians be given a viceregency." Only such a disposition
of higher administrative positions would allow the Muscovite boyar families to constrain high-born foreigners. Hence,
the only privilege the pact stipulated to the benefit of the
boyars fully coincided with the interests of the service class,
which above all feared for its patrimonies and service estates, "if foreigners should command the towns."

The middle service class apparently had some notion
of events in Poland. In this connection, interesting political
conversations transpired in Moscow between Poles and
Russians. "Unite with us," the Poles said, "and you, too,
shall have freedom." "Your freedom is dear to you,"
Russians answered them, "but our servitude is dear to us.
You have not liberty, but waywardness. The strong man
robs the weak and can deprive him of his estates and even
his life; yet under your laws it is difficult to cast judgment
upon such a person. The case can drag on for many years;
and in the end you take nothing from the offender. *But
among us the most distinguished boyar is not empowered
to harm the lowest commoner. On first complaint the Tsar
will pass judgment and take reprisal.* If the Tsar himself
acts unjustly, such is his liberty. But it is easier to bear injustice from the Tsar than from your own brother. For this
reason he is our common ruler."

Such speeches lead one to ask whether the democratic-
monarchic ideal of Ivashka Peresvetov had become a reality.
Or did the Muscovites perhaps contrast a Russian ideal with
the realities of life in Poland for reasons of patriotism, ignoring the facts of life in Russia? Whatever the answer, this
ideal obviously had now passed into the consciousness of
society. This has already been seen. It is again confirmed by
the indifference with which the middle service class accorded
to the boyars, *under the Tsar*, responsibility for new taxes
and for higher criminal justice and even control of the rights

of service people on their lands, "so that no one will realize
gain without merit or suffer loss without guilt."

Without a Tsar (or, more precisely, while awaiting a Tsar)
the calculations of the middle service class proved totally
incorrect. The provisional government of the boyars did not
abuse its power. On the contrary, the cause of all misfortune
was that, without the participation of "the entire land,"
its power proved to be too slight to countervail through its
authority further Polish claims on Russia. Sigismund found
the boyar government just as harmless as had the Muscovite
service people. Quickly Sigismund adulterated the staff of this
regime, adding his own sycophants. In this new form the
boyar government became a plaything in the hands of Gosiewski.[3] "You go to the boyars," Gosiewski was told concerning
his own activity in the *duma* at that time, "and bring a petition. You enter, seat yourself, then seat your advisers around
you. We cannot hear what you say and what you discuss
with your advisers. Whatever you wish done concerning any
petition, they do. The petitions are signed by those of
your advisers who are state secretaries." The service class
indeed suffered from these procedures, for the "petitions"
in which Gosiewski dictated his resolutions were chiefly direc-
tives concerning grants of land that were unlawfully large,
or given to those having no right to them whatsoever. In addition, the Muscovite provisional government, while in
Polish hands, intended to violate the imposed obligation "to
choose a sovereign of the entire land." Simultaneously,
the conditions by which the service class could advance a candidate were called into question, as was the identity of such
a candidate.

Thus the service class, for its own interests and those of
"the entire land" (which in this instance were identical)
had to create a new government. If the army men now strove
to place their newly created government *under the permanent control of the entire land*, they did so not from fear of
the strength of the class that had just betrayed complete

impotence, but because circumstances demanded a government
that was truly powerful. This fact explains the difference
between the new pact between the military men and Liapunov,
Trubetskoi and Zarutsky and the pact with Wladyslaw,
analyzed above. These two agreements do not express the
political aspirations of two diverse social strata. They are merely two formulations of the same political programs, their differences caused by the need to implement the old program under
changed political circumstances.

The more active role of the service people in the new government of Trubetskoi and his comrades primarily was expressed
in the conclusion (on June 30, 1611) of a formal agreement
with this government at the direct request of the middle service
class and at the insistence of their representative, Prokopy
Liapunov. Having learned from experience, the service people
concluded this agreement by reserving the right to replace
their elected representatives, should their activity cease to satisfy the requirements "of the entire land." That the decisions
of the middle service class were synonymous with the decisions
of the entire land no one now doubted. The new agreement
did not reiterate any of the fundamental questions of government
rights previously resolved by the agreement with Wladyslaw.
"The entire land" apparently continued to honor the conditions
it had elaborated since. For the moment it did not formally
renounce the candidate it had once nominated. But one of the
cardinal points of the agreement with Wladyslaw was given a
new wording in the verdict of June 30: governors chosen by the
land were to pledge "not to impose the death penalty on anyone nor to exile anyone in the towns without an announcement
to *the entire land*" (and not only to the boyars).

All the rest of this agreement refers to the termination of
the rapacious plundering of service lands sanctioned by the
Muscovite provisional government, through which Sigismund
had tried to recruit his own faction from among the Muscovite
service people. It is interesting that, while annulling all these decrees of the Muscovite government, the military men treated

with extreme leniency their own brothers who had profited from Polish generosity. Because they considered themselves the state, they felt no need to distinguish who among them were "straight" and who were "crooked." All who had been in Tushino, those who had been in Kaluga with the second Pretender, those who had served Tsar Vasily, those who had sworn allegiance to Wladyslaw, even those who had been in service to Sigismund (if perchance they had foresworn their patron in time) were all members of the same stratum. All had a right to their share of the service land.

The prime consideration was that some might not receive a just share, while others received too much. Such was the main concern and the primary interest of the class that dictated the agreement of June 30. This pact, as has been seen, was unconcerned with the basic problems of future governmental organization and did not once repeat the proposed obligation to secure the election of a sovereign of the entire land. Rather, it was completely absorbed in the most detailed measures that concerned the regulation of service landholding. Supervision of service and its remuneration were to be concentrated in central departments, and in the highest of these would sit the "highest of the middle service class," chosen by the entire land. Everything seized by service people would be returned to the treasury; and all service people in need or ruined would be recompensed. Runaway peasants would be returned to their owners, to the towns or to other landholders (for even at this critical moment the middle service class could not forget this sore point in its current economic situation). These were the essential features of the agreement. Whatever was not covered apparently was considered still to be regulated by previous enactments.

Only by accepting the view that the verdict of June 30 did not *repeal, but supplemented* the obligations assumed by "the entire land," is it possible correctly to understand its significance. The novelty was that "the entire land" henceforth thought it necessary to remain permanently attached to the mobilized militia as a constant "national council" [*zemskii sovet*].[4]   The goals were those of old; but the old method, by boyar representation of the land, had proven inadequate. Hereafter it was replaced by the new direct representation of the service class. Circumstances dictated that the assembly of the land [*zemskii sobor*] be promoted to replace the boyar *duma*.

There are grounds for believing that the agreement between the first popular militia and Trubetskoi was also binding upon the successors of both parties: the second popular militia and Pozharsky. Even if it was not renewed formally,[5] there truly was no need for renewal. "The entire land" that dispersed from the environs of Moscow after Liapunov's assassination[6] was the same "entire land" that had assumed the right to "change" its boyars and voevody by the agreement of June 30. The new representative of the land immediately recalled to the memory of the entire land the oath it had given: "to take general counsel with all the people and to choose a sovereign through general counsel with the advice of all the state." A convocation was ordered "of people of all ranks for a national council shortly thereafter." Having assembled in such full strength for the first time, the assembly of the land assumed all functions envisaged in the agreement between the military men and Trubetskoi. The assembly began, for example, to confiscate the palace lands bought up by service people with the help of the Muscovite provisional government, something that the agreement with Trubetskoi had stipulated directly. When an attempt was made on Pozharsky's life, the criminals were tortured *"by the entire army and the townspeople,"* then "were scattered throughout the towns and dungeons by *the land.*" Here was fulfilled a condition of the agreement noted earlier, "not to impose the death penalty on anyone or to exile anyone in the towns without an announcement to the entire land."

XI

**THE ASSEMBLY OF THE LAND AND THE
CRISIS OF AUTOCRACY**

How long did the new "national council" function under the
rights accorded it through the agreement with Trubetskoi
or transferred to it from the boyar provisional government,
whose role the council had to assume against its will? Was
there a moment when these functions were formally revoked
and the council's work was modestly limited to that of an
ordinary assembly of the land? These questions lead directly
to the explanation of a point that has remained controversial.
The question concerns the nature of the mutual relations
that were established between this assembly of the land and
the first Tsar of the new dynasty.

The answer to this question flows directly from an understanding of the significance of the previous pacts between
"the entire land" and the changing representatives of authority and candidates for the throne. Researchers seemingly
have erred in regarding each of these pacts as completely dis-
tinct from the others and, in studying their connection,
also have erred by seeking in each pact an expression of the
interests of a particular social group. But if all these proclamations are seen as being connected, as a series of statements constantly being adjusted to circumstances on behalf
of "the entire land" (that is, of one and only one class,
which grew ever more powerful as it became increasingly
organized), then the answer to this question becomes evident.
The surviving body of evidence concerning the agreement

between Michael Feodorovich and the entire land, and varied
other sources offering uniform testimony, provide confir-
mation. Once the content of this testimony is studied, conviction becomes still firmer.

The most reliable of these testimonies is that of Peter
the Great's contemporary, Vockerodt,[1] an observer who can
be faulted neither for intelligence nor for discernment. In
Vockerodt's words, "the magnates made themselves into a sort
of senate, which they called a *sobor*, and there not only the
boyars but also all other persons holding high governmental
positions (*welche in hohen Reichsbedienungen stunden*) sat and
had a voice. They reached a unanimous decision, not to choose
as Tsar anyone who would not promise them on oath fully to
promote justice in keeping with the ancient laws of the land;
not to judge or condemn anyone imperiously; not to introduce
new laws without the agreement of the *sobor*; not to aggra-
vate his subjects with new taxes, nor to make even the most
minute decision concerning military and civil matters (*in Kriegs-
und Friedensgeschaeften*). In order to bind the new Tsar more
firmly by these conditions, they resolved not to elect as their
lord anyone belonging to an influential family or having many
followers, with whose help he might violate the laws prescribed for him and return once again to supreme power. Tsar
Michael signed these conditions without hesitation, and for
a time the government was conducted in the prescribed manner."

Except for the information concerning the choice of the
"family" to which the Tsar was to belong, Vockerodt's
reports contain nothing new. The conditions imposed upon
Michael were precisely the same as those proposed to Wladyslaw, except that the *sobor* was substituted for the boyar
duma, and "not only boyars," but others as well were to participate. But this change had really been made in the earlier
agreements, as is known from the pact between the middle
service class and Trubetskoi. Whether this agreement was renewed formally with Pozharsky is unknown. But even if
there was no new agreement, it can be assumed that the old

agreement remained in force. Obviously Pozharsky considered himself bound by some of the resolutions of the old agreement, and the most important ones at that.

Vockerodt has described somewhat vaguely the institution through which restrictions on power were introduced. Yet even here he remained faithful to the truth. We know that the "military council" [*ratnyi sovet*] attached to the militias, having reached an agreement with their leaders, did cease to resemble a *duma* but had not yet acquired the character of a full assembly of the land. Ostensibly, this council contained "not only boyars," but "all ranks" attended, though only on paper. What is no less correct (and is very crucial to Vockerodt's account) is that the military council introduced conditions elaborated beforehand, before the selection of a personal candidate. This must have been so, for the conditions proposed to Michael were identical to those proposed earlier to Wladyslaw, then altered, because the course of events replaced the Muscovite boyar government with the institution of "the entire land," which superceded the boyars as to rights and obligation. Vockerodt's testimony in all its nuances fits the historical situation of the moment to which it refers.

But even as early as the seventeenth century the memory of the Russian people recorded this event with a shading that was one-sided and incorrect, thereby fully justifying the doubts that have been created among researchers. These scholars erred only in that, instead of questioning how this fact had been *appraised* by Russian sources, they questioned *the fact itself*. As this circumstance is recorded by the chronicle of Pskov and by Kotoshikhin,[2] it seems to repeat the history of Tsar Vasily Shuisky. The *boyars* had made it incumbent upon the Tsar to put to death no one without a trial and without guilt, or to do anything without *the counsel of the boyars.* But circumstances were such when the new Tsar was elected that the boyars were powerless and unable to impose any obligations. They became as much of an object of animosity by "the entire land" as had the Cossacks. And "the entire land" was omnipotent at that time through its army and its representatives in the assembly of the land.

The role played by the assembly of the land during the last months of the Time of Troubles and the first decade of the reign of Michael Feodorovich conclusively demonstrates that we have understood this matter rationally. This role was wholly exceptional. The assembly now changed from an institution convened in *exceptional* cases for *deliberative* voting on *only those* questions addressed to it by the ruling power, into a standing institution in continuous session, with a permanent staff of deputies that changed every three years. The assembly covered a broad range of business that was not only legislative and constitutive in character but also purely administrative. This institution communicated directly with the provincial administration of its own accord. In short, during these extraordinary times it actually managed "the most minute" (*die allergeringsten*) matters of war and peace." The customary formula for announcing laws and decrees, "the Sovereign has decreed, and the boyars have resolved," was altered temporarily to another form: "We, the Great Sovereign, have spoken and explained in the assembly, and the military men and the elected representatives of all the people of all the Great Russian states (or towns) have resolved." In cases of particular importance the people of all ranks even affixed their own signatures to such "decrees of the Sovereign and resolutions of the entire land," "so that our (notarized) promise would have the consent of you (the land)."

Vockerodt again proved to be completely correct in another of his reports. The system just described actually functioned for a very brief time, only "as long as the Sovereign's father, Filaret, had not returned from captivity in Poland." In 1619 Filaret Romanov arrived in Moscow;[3] and in 1622 the regular (third) session of the permanent assembly of the land ended. With the collaboration of this session Filaret fulfilled one of the most important commitments that had been imposed upon Wladyslaw, the obligation to register the losses of service people in districts devastated during the Time of Troubles and to grant them tax advantages. Thereafter Filaret no longer summoned new deputies. Ten years later he even embarked upon the Polish War without asking permission from "the entire land."[4] But this war was protracted and demanded additional, unforeseen military expenditures. It became necessary to make the entire land tax itself once again. In 1633 and 1634 an assembly of the land once again appeared on the scene.

Three or four years later the same story was repeated. Again the government attempted to function without the help of the assembly, and once more it failed and had to summon an assembly to prescribe a new tax and a new levy for the entire land. Yet little more than half the money formally promised by the deputies was collected successfully. It can be imagined what the gathering of taxes and recruits would have yielded, had the government had to rely upon its own resources. For this reason the assembly of the land was still needed by the government.

Having learned from bitter experience, the state rulers dealt more seriously with the question of whether or not to wage war when that question arose for a third time following the Cossacks' capture of Azov in 1642. The "ranks" of the entire land were convoked with particularly full representation, and their opinions were presented with special care and detail "in a letter." The government asked whether a rupture with the Turks and the Tsar of the Crimea should be forced, and, if so, where the government could secure the resources for such a war, which promised to be quite prolonged. The deputies, who were predominantly drawn from those strata of society upon which depended the punctuality of payments, answered that they were unable to pay. Azov was abandoned.

XII

THE RISE OF THE BUREAUCRACY

At last "the entire land" had decided a question of war or peace. Now for the first time a new note was heard in the voice of the entire land: "We are being ruined by Muscovite red tape and by unjust courts, more than by the Turks and the Crimean Moslems," protested the representatives of the middle service class of the towns. "Our brothers," the middle service class of the towns, go to Moscow as officials ("on government business"); while serving in the offices [*prikazy*] and the provisional government they grow rich, while the military service suffers. The sovereign's courtiers also occupy profitable positions in governing crown properties and neglect to serve in the regiments. State secretaries and under-secretaries busy themselves with "government affairs," accept bribes and acquire "indescribable mansions" that under former sovereigns even "highborn" people could not own. Merchants added that they suffered because of the voevody: "Under former sovereigns the elected elder managed things in the towns, and townspeople were tried among neighbors, and there were no voevody in the towns. Voevody and their soldiers were sent only to frontier towns to guard against the Turks, the Crimeans and the Nogais."[1] Finally, even the lowly taxed people of the Muscovite tax-administered settlements [*chernye slobody*][2] complained that the sovereign harnessed them to service; as sworn men[3] in government offices and as "lower police servitors"[4] in the fire-fighting forces and the Muscovite police.

All these expressions of displeasure from the great and the small had the same meaning. Precisely when "the entire land" had escaped from the boyars and Cossacks through its own direct effort and strove to restore the "former customs" of the Muscovite state under the supervision of its deputies, there arose an evil that was not new in its essence but in its dimensions. An evil appeared that seemed very much part of the very goal for which the land was striving, that is, the restoration of public order. Against this unexpected enemy "the land," in turn, proved powerless. This enemy was the Muscovite bureaucracy.

The Time of Troubles had been accompanied by the total destruction of government and the absence of regular administration. This state of affairs necessitated a permanent assembly of the land. Naturally, reorganization of government was the first measure that Filaret, the father of the sovereign, had to adopt when he undertook to "build the state anew." He set to work on this task with his customary energy and skill. The result of his efforts was a strongly bureaucratic system that undoubtedly restored order to government affairs, while sparing the authorities the need to consult the opinion of "all ranks" on every important occasion. The newly imposed governmental system returned the state to the hands of the all-powerful bureaucracy, virtually a ruling stratum over whose abuses no real control was possible.

It happened that the very class that several years earlier had legislated and commanded in its own name immediately thereafter was reduced to expressing its helpless complaints before state officials. How could this class have allowed itself to undergo a change so disadvantageous to its interests? The answer lies in the views (which we have already seen to some extent) of the service class concerning the role that had become its lot because of the events of the Time of Troubles. The service class had imagined that this role would be temporary and extraordinary. Never did it wish to establish a new system of government through its agreements with its representatives

elected positions of authority. This the service class regarded
merely as the quickest way to reinstate "former customs."
Its main objective was "that after the destruction of Muscovy
the Russian state should never in the future be without a
sovereign." Thus it feared not an excess of power but an in-
sufficiency of power, and adopted measures against this.
Here is why, instead of organizing regular control over the state
authority and ensuring the effectiveness of such control, the
service class dared not become the government in order to re-
lieve the transient weakness of the ruling power. When the
moment of weakness passed, it immediately and without protest terminated participation in the government and surren-
dered all hope of control. From its own viewpoint, the service
class even then had remained in the government too long.

The service people always regarded their powers as deputies an unpleasant duty to be dispensed as late as possible
and to be rendered as quickly as possible. The service class
developed neither a taste for power nor a need for power
during the few years of its ordeals with the militia and the assemblies of the land. More adroit members of this class used
their proximity to the court and the government to become
established "in government business." But the bulk of the service class strove to take advantage of this brief interlude in
power nearer home, in the local countryside, where service people consolidated their economic position in their own localities.
To secure the future political power of this class was never
seriously considered, for the service class was still too poorly
organized and too devoid of political sense. The political views
of their majority coincided with the notions expressed during
the discussions between the Poles and Russians in Moscow,
cited above. A century would pass before this situation changed.

All this leads to the conclusion that the consciousness of
this class, which had not yet progressed from the idea of service
to the notion of supremacy, offers no reason to search for elements of opposition or criticism. The substance of the "service"
mentality was limited to the nationalistic ideologies already

mentioned. Critical political attitudes in the seventeenth century cannot be found in class struggles, as was true of the phenomena of the fifteenth century. These elements must be discovered in the bureaucracy and in the influx of foreign ideas that stirred the bureaucracy to action.

XIII

**IMPACT OF THE WEST UPON RUSSIAN
NATIONAL SELF-CONSCIOUSNESS**

Russian nationalists have always considered the seventeenth century the epoch of the fullest flowering of national ideals. Russian Westernizers have seen this century as a period of preparation for the Petrine reforms, that is, the Europeanization of Russia. Both are equally correct. These two assertions are not two conflicting and mutually exclusive attitudes but two sides of the same truth, mutually connected in most intimate manner. During the seventeenth century the first slanting rays of European enlightenment began to gild the crests of Russian society. The bare, dry trunks upon which these crests splendidly blossomed cast long shadows. The shadows, indistinguishable in color, represent the reflection in social consciousness of national originality.

A comparison drawn from the field of amateur photography perhaps explains our thought still better. A photographic plate that has been exposed is full of figures and forms, shadows and light, yet seems just as clear and smooth as before. But once this plate is immersed in a certain chemical solution, its inner contents begin to appear. At first sky and horizon are obscured by a thick, dark shadow. Against

this background white silhouettes sharply emerge, though still
lacking detail. Then, sharp, black features appear here and
there in the white areas. These are followed by half-tones; and
finally everything blends into a single, whole picture. The picture had actually been prepared before its "development" in
the solution. But every photographer understands that not only
is a "developer" needed to reveal the picture, but that to some
extent the distribution of color and shadow in the picture can
be affected by modifying the composition of the chemical
solution.

Foreign influence generally plays the role of "developer"
of the picture created by history, the picture of a definite
national type. Before this reagent begins to function, a nation
is as little conscious of its own nationality as Moliere's hero
was aware that he spoke prose. In the social psyche, as in the
individual psyche, consciousness arises as a result of contrast.
Wherever contrast can be detected more quickly and easily
(as in small tribal groups, among mixed populations, in frontier
districts and the like), consciousness of national differences
emerges more rapidly and assumes sharper forms. But in a
country such as continental Russia national self-consciousness
must develop late and slowly. Even once developed, it often
seems not an instinct, but an abstract idea. Leaders of the
common people consider it a paroxysm, while the people themselves deem it a factor not always advantageous.

The sequence by which national consciousness arises
strikes something of a parallel with our example from photography. Again there is a sharp difference between the black
background of foreign nationalism and the white contour of
native nationalism, the difference that first and foremost
registers in the consciousness. The point of departure for national consciousness is usually religious in form. To the
sociologist religious faith certainly is not what it is to the
theologian, not the totality of revealed truths that are often
poorly known and even poorly understandable by the people, but a banner familiar to all, accessible and distinguishable,

around which surges the struggle for national exclusiveness.
In this sense faith and nationalism naturally must become identical conceptions that are inseparable. Whoever supports
"the faith" thereby supports nationalism, with the former, more
obvious notion now replaced by one more abstract.

Undoubtedly this precise meaning was inherent in all de-
clarations of this sort uttered by those who lived during the
Time of Troubles, the first paroxysm of Russian national self-
consciousness and the first broad, popular realization of the
contrast between what was native and what was foreign. Changing one's faith was just as physically impossible as changing
one's "nature." Russians were nonplussed by such happenings
as, for example, the conversion of a Russian youth sent abroad
by Boris Godunov to study languages under an English pastor.[1]
Russians simply refused to believe such a conversion possible.
They assumed that the English had forcibly compelled the
Russian student to alter his faith and were even prepared to
believe that his faith had been "enticed away from the youth."
But that he should voluntarily refuse to return to his homeland? "It is impossible to leave the Orthodox faith and to forget one's native state, his Sovereign, his mothers, his family
and his people." *"But how can he forget his nature?,"* Russian
ambassadors asked the English government. For twenty years
they insisted that their prodigal son be returned to Russia.

What sort of national significance was concealed beneath
this religious symbol? What kind of individual features were
united by this common tie, this white contour of religion?
When did the individual features that filled in the contours begin to "develop" in consciousness? Further work by the
"developer" was needed to raise to consciousness the contents
of this symbol. Customs, a way of life, certain features of
life, surroundings and character could be appreciated as dis-
tinctively national only when, paralleling yet simultaneously
contrasting them, features of foreign custom and a foreign
way of life were juxtaposed in close proximity. This had not
happened to any significant extent until the seventeenth

century. Hence, the filling-in of the bare religious contours of
national self-consciousness with the vital features of life could
be the accomplishment only of the seventeenth century. It is
also natural that the Russian way of life should remain impressed upon national consciousness in exactly the form in
which it had arisen at the moment of its "development," in the
seventeenth century.

The way of life that then had developed most fully and
had begun to grow obsolete contained much, of course, that
was far from original and national. In earlier ages, when the
notion of a national pattern of life had not yet emerged, very
many individual features of foreign ways of life had, like smug-
glers, successively stolen into the structure of national life
and had been given national sanction. More than a few of the
foreign elements that had been adopted earlier, when nationalism had developed unconsciously, now passed for what was
native. If we distinguish the foreign elements assumed to be
native from those that still bore their import stamp in the
general consciousness, we can determine exactly, in every dis-
tinct sphere of life, where lay the boundary between the
periods of unconscious and conscious national development.

An objection might be offered that all this is simply a
matter of time. Time passes, and what has been adopted
recently also becomes a thing adopted long ago; the consciousness of its foreign origins will be lost as well, just as consciousness of the origins of Russia's way of life in the seventeenth
century was lost. This is absolutely correct. But this cannot
prevent the contention that in various eras of national history,
as in the various ages of any man, the ability to remember
the past also differs. The memory of society, like the individual
memory, is moulded and strengthened at a certain time in the
historical life of a people. All that precedes this moment preserves no memory, or an extremely vague memory, of itself.
Everything that occurs on this side of the dividing line forms a
more or less unbroken thread of associated remembrances,
while the technical means of preserving these remembrances

are ever more perfected. But on the far side remains the legacy inherited from the first, unconscious period of historical life by the second, which is conscious. This legacy usually constitutes the *nationalistic tradition.*

Such an origin of the nationalistic tradition is explained by the fact that the contents of this tradition are primordial and incapable of analysis. Within the historical memory of a people these contents are indeed so. But this memory is much shorter than the historical life of a people. However, history, which corrects and augments this memory, discovers ways to display the nationalistic tradition in its component parts and to search out its sources. For this reason the nationalistic tradition has no greater enemy than history.

The preceding chapters have engaged in precisely such an historical analysis of the origin of Russian nationalistic tradition. This analysis led to the conclusion that even during the initial formulation of nationalistic ideals foreign influences played the main, even the decisive role. This is why elements of the national tradition, even at its very beginning, were connected closely and directly with elements of criticism. Ivan the Terrible, who gave national ideals such an effective sanction, in conversation with a foreigner could not find words sufficiently harsh to describe the low moral level of his subjects. But when his collocutor was bewildered and reminded the Tsar that he was a Russian himself, Ivan resolutely retorted that he was not a Russian at all, but a German, for he was descended from Prus. It is hardly surprising that later nationalists, as early as the seventeenth century, censured Ivan IV for his westernism instead of worshipping him as a national hero of popular legend, as shall be seen below.

The elements of criticism were also destined to develop more fully in these same surroundings, that is, among representatives of the court and the government. Positive as well as negative causes were equally responsible for this circumstance. One negative factor was the absence in Russia of any other social group that could become the bearer of an

oppositional, critical ideology. The events of the Time of
Troubles demonstrate this truth. A positive cause was this,
that the direct source of criticism, foreign influence, was
more immediate and accessible to the court and the higher
bureaucracy. Consequently these strata had to give the
nationalistic ideology its formal formulation.

The immediate task is that of determining the power
of the foreign reagent and describing the reaction it pro-
voked. In other words, we must first trace the diffusion of
foreign ideas and the foreign mode of life during the seventeenth century, then define the significance that the elements
of criticism enjoyed, not in destroying nationalistic ideals
(for the time for that had not yet come) but in defining the
nationalistic ideal more fully and more exactly for the first
time.

XIV

WESTERN INFLUENCES IN EVERYDAY LIFE

At first the influence of foreign culture had to exhibit a character more material than ideological. Before the influence of
western *ideas* was felt, Russian life was affected by the influence of the western *way of life*, the influence of higher culture and then (or, more correctly, along with this) the impact
of European applied and technical knowledge. The first
seemed innocuous, while the second was required by immediate necessity. In both instances European influence became part of Russian life spontaneously, gradually and unob-
trusively, initally arousing only comparatively weak and powerless protest. Meanwhile both European life and European

technical knowledge drew Russians unconsciously into the circle of European ideas and conceptions. When Russians finally regained their consciousness of the unexpectedly large total of foreign customs that had been adopted little by little, it was too late to retreat. The old way of life had been virtually destroyed. There was no recourse but to make the past the subject of a nationalistic cult and abstract idealization.

In the seventeenth century the spontaneous process by which the foreign way of life influenced Russia had just begun. Even in matters of everyday life the successes won by foreign influences were very limited, were achieved slowly and spread only among a very narrow social circle. In the Tsar's palace and in several of the more aristocratic homes of Moscow there appeared various examples of European furniture, which, it is true, did not supplant but merely supplemented the old. Side by side with the simple, plain tables of faked or oak wood could be found tables "in the Polish style" or "of German workmanship," of "ebony" or "Indian" wood, with legs that were curved or finely moulded with carving. Side by side with the traditional wall benches stood armchairs of intricate upholstery and "gilded German" chairs, which by the end of the century could be purchased on Ovoshchny Riad[1] in Moscow at a ruble apiece (in prices of that time).

Wall mirrors also appeared, though only in interior living rooms at first. These, however, were hung with taffeta or were covered, like an icon-case, by bars in order to stress their utilitarian and not their aesthetic role. Table clocks and pocket watches gained the same prominence and from the beginning of the seventeenth century had become articles of fairly common use, as can be judged from the comparatively large number of freely practicing clockmakers who seemingly won for themselves sufficient subsistence in Moscow at the time.

The pictures that gradually supplanted murals by the end of the century undoubtedly enjoyed some aesthetic value. These pictures imitated the traditional content of the murals:

largely scenes from Church history or, more rarely, simply historical or allegorical themes. One novelty was the portrayal of "persons from life," that is, portrait paintings. Pictures of this sort were, of course, a luxury not to be enjoyed by many. For broader audiences these pictures were replaced by cheap engravings, the "Italian sheets" of foreign craftsmanship and their Russian reproductions. By the end of the century the printing of engravings had become part of the local industry that flourished in Moscow and Kiev and supplied with its wares the merchants of Moscow's Ovoshchny Riad and the Spassky Gates. Their cheapness (from a half kopeck to two kopecks at the time) and their variety of subject matter, sometimes very serious, more often moral or religious and often even ridiculous, inspired demand for these "Italian sheets," the precursors of our cheap popular prints, among ever broader audiences. In the homes of the wealthy these sheets could be seen in hundreds, while in the palace they occasionally replaced wallpaper. Bit by bit the traditional Russian cottage was converted into a mansion. But at first this conversion was restricted to true mansions.

Polish and German influence upon dress took root more quickly than did foreign furniture. One could cite many items of dress that undoubtedly had been borrowed, then converted to "native" national property by the time that massive adoptions began in the seventeenth century. As early as the end of the fifteenth century a local pastor of the frontier town of Pskov had exhorted his flock "not to wear German dress."[2] In the middle of the sixteenth century the pamphlet already mentioned, the "Dialogues of Sergei and German," again censured sinners "who covet the chasubles of sinners that stretch from head to foot" and even threatened "grief" to all members of the "Christian family who become attracted to the trousers and hats of unbelievers and wear these things themselves." Throughout the entire seventeenth century extends a series of accusations and prohibitions that apparently were as impotent as their predecessors. As early as the days of Michael Feodorovich the Tsar's children wore German dress tailored for them by their tutor,

Morozov.[3] In 1675 a special decree forbade use of such dress
by the service ranks that filled the palace. The Tsar reduced
one court youth to lower rank for wearing a stylish hairdo, and
this occasioned the decree just mentioned, that court ranks
(*stol'niki, striapchie, dvoriane and zhil'tsy*) "should not adopt
the foreign customs of Germans and others; they should not
trim their hair and also should not wear gowns, caftans and
caps. They should also order their slaves not to wear them."
Yet at the same time and thereafter Polish and German tailors
freely plied their trade in the stalls of Moscow, apparently
finding a clientele. The Tsarist decree at most merely succeeded
in temporarily compelling Muscovite dandies to refrain from
becoming an eyesore at court because of their new fashions.

It was much more difficult for new influences to affect
traditional pastimes than had been the case with furniture and
dress. The strict order of Russian life, which was regulated in
detail, turned life into a ritual that had to be observed, at least
on the average, no less than did the rites of religion. Yet even
here a loop-hole could be found. A weakly defended point
appeared, through which new trends pierced a path into the
Russian mind and heart. The sole moment of the day when
the Russian was left to himself, when neither faith nor society
nor even household procedure demanded anything of him
were the hours (long enough, to be sure) devoted to repose.
The Russian used this interval of rest to become undisciplined
of will and to violate systematically all that he had been constrained to observe so strictly throughout the rest of the day.
Earlier he had been sensible; now he permitted himself to
act the fool. Earlier he had been humble; now he humbled
and bullied others. Earlier he had been a true servant of the
Church; now he regressed to his pagan past, stubbornly
ignoring all the precepts of the Church. This leisure time
provided a sanctuary for the popular literature suppressed
by the Church. At least fragments of this literature were
rescued from ruin. Now the mask of meekness and humility
was cast aside and there freely resounded the laughter that
strict moralists regarded the start of spiritual ruin.

If a man did not launch into singing and dancing amid all this revelry, it was merely because he had to maintain his dignity before his menials. In compensation he forced others to sing, dance and do all sorts of humorous things to their heart's content, and the more complicated, the more racy, the more cynical, the better. Here, in short, was a kingdom of fools and idiots, of "braggards" (story-tellers) and "domra players"[4] (tellers of epics to the sounds of the domra) that became a set feature in the home of every rich Russian during the hours of repose after dinner or before retiring. In this sector, which was most poorly defended, the foreign "Polish" or "German" amusements could be implanted more easily and less conspicuously.

The first pioneers of this foreign invasion were touring acrobats, jugglers and clowns. One of these, the "German" Ivan Semenov, for ten consecutive years entertained the family of Tsar Michael Feodorovich in the "Amusement Palace" and left behind him an entire school of students. "He taught five men to walk along ropes and to dance and all sorts of fun that he knew; he also taught 24 men to beat on drums."[5] From the beginning of the seventeenth century there was an abundance of foreign musicians at the Muscovite court. Even during the sixteenth century organs and cymbals (that is, a type of piano) figured in the court inventory.

But with the coronation of Alexis Mikhailovich the growth of all these court amusements came to an end. Instead of epics and tales by "braggards" and "domra players," the sovereign's "poverty-stricken pilgrims" sang spiritual hymns "to heaven" in his presence. Instead of organ playing Alexis maintained a harmonious church choir. Musical instruments and masks were subjected to a solemn auto-da-fe[6] outside of Moscow, at Bolota. The Tsar quit the "Amusement Palace" for merrymaking with bears and for his favorite sports, falconry and the chase.

This abstention from foreign and pagan amusements lasted, however, only as long as Tsar Alexis' first wife was alive.

Upon his marriage to his second wife, Natalia Kirillovna, who had been emancipated by Matveev,[7] the court seemed to hasten to make up for lost time and immediately turned to the most complex form of foreign amusement, theatrical performances. This was in 1672-1675. The theatre was a form new to Russia but, inasmuch as all that comprised it was old, transition to this new form did not occasion special protest. Theatrical performances slipped by under the guise of "scenes from the Bible," that is, the reenactment by characters of well-known Biblical subjects: Esther, Tobias, Judith and Joseph. The "Deeds of Temir-Aksakovo" was the only timid attempt to depart from the circle of Biblical themes to the realm of history. Yet even here the author contrived to depict the hero (Tamerlane) as a Christian zealot of the faith.[8]

Beneath this disguise, of course, contraband was concealed: the romantic and humorous element that was prohibited by the Church. But this prohibition had been violated too often in the past. The audience recognized on the stage essentially the same fools and idiots with their stupid jokes and blunt cynicism. The impudent realism of the amorous conversations between Holophernes and Judith or between Potiphar's wife and Joseph hardly scandalized contemporary tastes. One factor served to explain the success of these first theatrical endeavors. Their organizers adapted to the Russian stage not a new repertoire from the German theatre, which had then been rejuvenated, but old rags that had been worn out by itinerant German actors at fairs after having been accommodated to the lowest standards. The wit of the Dutch Pickelhering[9] and the sensuality of "English comedy" were just the thing for the court audience of Moscow. There were more than enough military scenes, commotion and thunder, fighting and killing in these comedies to satisfy the most exacting lover of farce. In short, the novelty was suited to tastes.

Foreign artists at court also proved useful. A painter drew scenes "by drawing in perspective," three dozen at a time. An organist formed an orchestra with the help of Matveev's

court musicians. A German pastor from the "foreign settlement" directed and trained actors. He also selected plays to be
translated, apparently by clerks from the Foreign Office
[*Posol'skii prikaz*]. Hence, to carry on this new undertaking
all resources then on hand in Moscow were utilized. The
result surpassed expectations. For three years in succession
performances did not cease in winter or in summer. Actors,
orchestra and scenery moved with the Tsar and his court
from the Kremlin Palace to Preobrazhenskoe[10] and back again.

The foreign influences of the seventeenth century were
not limited to outward changes in the way of life, and to furniture and the pastimes of notable people. As early as the
middle of the century the Muscovite government, because of
influence that was partly Polish and partly Greek, began to
examine critically the religious ideologies of the nationalists
of the sixteenth century. The result of this scrutiny was a dispute between representatives of the official Church and the
defenders of the national'ideology, who quickly communicated
their oppositionist mood to the Russian people.

But after they had mastered religious nationalism, the
Muscovite authorities stopped halfway. Soon they had to
defend the religion they had just liberated from its old
nationalistic content against new trends, Polish and European
in nature. We know that the struggle against these new
trends, however, was just as much beyond their strength as
had been the struggle against religious nationalism. Pure for-
malism could satisfy neither those who wished to live by
their old hopes for a messianic role for the Russian people nor
those who, enamored of European tendencies or the needs
of their own hearts, sought new forms of religious thought and
feeling. As a result, both thought and feeling slipped away
from the authority of official leaders. The old faith, on one
hand, and rationalism and mysticism, on the other, found the
soil prepared for their dissemination by the end of the century.

Even fewer obstacles were encountered by European
secular knowledge, when it first appeared as scraps of outdated

medieval learning transmitted through Poland, then assumed its true form. There is no need to return now to all the consequences of these foreign influences. At this point the positive content of the stock of new ideas and sentiments transmitted to Russia is more interesting to this study than the process by which these ideas and sentiments were passed on and the consciousness they aroused of the contrast between nationalism and Europeanism. This theme, the ways and means of European ideological influence and its impact on national consciousness, must now be investigated.

XV

THE FOREIGNER IN SEVENTEENTH-CENTURY RUSSIA

The chief manner in which the influence of European ideas penetrated Russia, of course, was direct contact between Russians and foreigners, at home or abroad. Before the end of the seventeenth century journeys abroad by Russians were a rare and exceptional happening. Godunov's first attempt to send Russians abroad for training ended, as seen, in complete failure. The youths proved more susceptible to the advantages of European culture than the Muscovite government had intended. Thereafter Moscow grew extremely wary of foreign trips. Only foreigners who had been acclimatized in Russia and their sons were permitted such travel, while Russians were unconditionally prohibited to journey abroad. One of the first few Russian emigrants to violate this prohibition was Kotoshikhin, who fled to Sweden to escape Muscovite ways. Kotoshikhin has recorded in perfect truthfulness the considerations that motivated the government.

"They do not send their children to other states for knowledge
and training," he said, "for fear that once they have learned
the faith and customs and happy liberty of those states, they
will begin to disaffirm their own faith and adhere to others, and
will have no care or thought of returning to their own homes
and relatives." Thus those who would most benefit from such
a journey were unable to go abroad.

From time to time a Russian embassy did appear in
Europe. But these Muscovite officials, who had become impro-
vised diplomats by the will of their government, were the
least prepared for the role of observing European life. Unac-
quainted with languages, haphazardly reading their official
speeches word for word from a notebook, they were preoccupied by one thing only: not to take any step or utter any
word that would detract from the honor of their state and expose themselves to official punishment. Occasionally they
had no objection to enjoying the unaccustomed freedom of
living, but how they interpreted this freedom brought repugnance to those who chanced to witness their debauchery. To
the eyes of European observers, their actions were not even
"barbarism," but simple "bestiality" and "swinishness."

The pleasures of the European manner, as well as the de-
lights of travel—scenes of nature, monuments of art, the
acquisition of culture—were separated from them by the Chi-
nese wall created by their intellectual and moral coarseness.
Wherever they appeared, they were accompanied by their own
atmosphere, literally and figuratively. Lodgings where they
had rested had to be ventilated and cleaned for almost an entire week. Their appearance on the street, in brocades and silk
of red, yellow or green, in full-length oriental robes with regal
collars and extremely long sleeves, with fur caps of Asiatic
style, drew to them a gaping crowd. They seemed either a mas-
querade, or a religious procession, or simply an ethnographic
curiosity exported from foreign lands by some enterprising
entrepreneur, along with crocodiles from the Nile and African
lions. When Moscow finally understood by the end of the

seventeenth century what sort of impression these half-baked
diplomats were making abroad, they were replaced by foreigners who had made their homes in Russia. The worldly experience and secular spirit of the latter thereupon caused
amazement in European diplomatic circles, which had grown
accustomed to thinking of *grobianita Muscovitica* [Musco-
vite coarseness].

Travel abroad could therefore accomplish nothing, or
next to nothing, to strengthen foreign influence in Russia.
But the direct collision of Russians and foreigners at home
had a significance far different. The history of such collision began very long ago and need not be retraced from its
beginnings. As long as the foreign element trickled into
Russian life only in isolated rivulets, it was swept away by the
current or sank to the bottom, assimilated by its surroundings
and vanishing impotently from the surface of life. Only when
the immigration of foreigners reached greater numerical
proportions did isolated individuals begin to linger ever longer
on the surface, clinging to and supporting each other, so
that by the end of the seventeenth century there was formed
in Moscow a large and well organized colony, a small oasis
of Europe amid a cultural desert.

Historical sources speak of the first origins of this colony
as early as the first half of the sixteenth century. Herber-
stein recounts that Vasily III appointed for his bodyguards
(chosen from Lithuanians and Poles) a special settlement for
them to occupy, Nalivka, the name of which is still preserved
in the name of a church between Polianka and Yakimanka.
Researchers explain the subsequent disappearance of this first
foreign settlement as due to the raid of Devlet-Girei[1] in 1571.
It is more reasonable to conjecture that this corps of bodyguards simply became Russified gradually and remained in
place, although reorganized and under a new name, *streltsy*,[2]
which was bestowed upon them by Ivan the Terrible in the
1560s.

The 1560s also witnessed a new and massive influx of foreigners. Following the Livonian campaigns,[3] thousands of prisoners were introduced to Russia. Some of them were dispersed throughout various provincial towns, where the majority of them again apparently remained too long and were Russified. Others were settled in the capital. A new location was set aside for them, near the mouth of the Yauza River, on its right bank. Like the old "foreign" settlement, the new one was free from excise duty on spirits; and its inhabitants quickly grew rich from the sale of wine. In 1578 this foreign settlement fell victim to one of Ivan the Terrible's fits of anger. He ordered it subjected to an outright assault and to be pillaged. But the colony on the Yauza soon recovered from this pogrom and by the end of the century seemed to reach its greatest prosperity, thanks to Godunov's considerate attitude toward foreigners. During the Time of Troubles, however, the foreign settlement was burned and lay deserted an entire half century. Its populace was scattered throughout various districts and a goodly number of them remained there henceforth.

But this did not check the growth of the number of foreigners in Moscow. On the contrary, when deprived of their settled way of life in the suburb of Yauza, the foreigners relocated their settlements to Moscow itself and remained there until mid-century, continually increasing in number. Instead of their former single church, which had been Lutheran, they now had two, one of which was Reformed. Their main center was the Petrovka and Chistye Prudy sections of the city. But their homes, for which they outbid local inhabitants, also sprung up in the Tversky, Arbat and Sivtsevyi Vrazhok sections. Scattered among Russians, the foreigners little by little involuntarily grew accustomed to Russian life. They came to know Russians, kept Russian domestics, adopted the language and, in the end, even wore Russian dress to attract less attention in town.

This aroused the apprehension of Russian merchants, for whom foreigners knocked down the price of goods, homeowners, for whom foreigners drove up the price of land, and the clergy, who began to fear foreign influences upon morals. A series of complaints were filed, which the government felt obliged to satisfy. Among the measures to be mentioned below was one radical enactment against foreigners that marks the end of an era in the history of their community. Foreigners were ordered to sell their homes to Russian proprietors. Foreign churches within the city were torn down. A place was set aside for a resettlement of the foreign colony, "where the foreign households had been before," that is, on the Yauza River, but somewhat upstream. In this manner the final location of the "New Foreign" Settlement was determined in 1652, in the area where Nemetskaia Street is today.

Expulsion of foreigners from the city limits achieved its goal. The blending of foreigners and Russians was halted. Yet the force of foreign influence simultaneously increased, for now beneath the very walls of the capital there arose a small foreign town with a style of life and customs that was utterly unique. Hitherto foreigners had feared assimilation by the Russian element far more than Russians had been threatened by the adoption of foreign culture. Now this culture stood next door, in all its inviolability, as a model always ready for imitation. Representatives of Muscovite authority had wished to prevent the amalgamation of Russian and foreign ways of life. Now they had to experience a time when Moscow was dominated culturally by the Foreign Settlement.

There is no need to preserve any unusually high opinion of the standard of culture among those assembled in the Foreign Settlement. The motto of its populace was the same as that formulated in a Latin verse by one of its pastors, Berg: *omne solum forti est, ut piscibus aequor*; that is, "Any place is the fatherland of the bold, as the sea is for the fish." The populace suffered no lack of adventurers, or lovers of easy profit. Here were more than a few charlatans, skillfully exploiting Russian ignorance to sell cheap services at a high price. As usual, this ubiquitous army of volunteer civilizers, who invariably appear in all countries lacking culture, made more noise and caused more scandal than all the rest. They attracted to the entire colony the hatred of the local population (whom they outbid in their prices for grain) and created for the colony the worst possible reputation.

Naturally not every member of the Foreign Settlement was of this sort. Especially in secondary and tertiary positions could be found not a few men like, for example, Falck, a specialist in cannon-making, who during one of the scandalous trials in the settlement gave his sullen testimony that "he did not associate with intriguers, for he was not an idle man." Such people, who sought little, brought their labor and knowledge to an alien land and performed their humble work with honor.

Initially all types, charlatans and honest toilers alike, were beneficial to Russian culture. Professional men among the foreign populace were fully employed to serve the needs of the sovereign and his government. At first the needs of the sovereign were paramount. A foreign physician had long been part of the Muscovite court. He was followed by specialists in gold and silver work, "organ players," painters and the like. The needs of the government were met by interpreters in the Foreign Office, who were also the first translators of serious foreign literature. Regimental doctors were very few in number. There were also skilled specialists in military affairs and related fields. If the rather sizable element of commercial people who settled in Moscow for their own interests are added to this list, the composition of the oldest foreign community is complete, for common soldiers should not be numbered among this group of foreign intelligentsia.

With the passage of time the military faction swelled to ever greater size and finally occupied first place in the ranks of the foreign aristocracy. As early as the 1630s Colonel Leslie and his fellow officers appeared, to reorganize the Russian armed forces for war with Poland (unsuccessfully, by the way).

Under Leslie's command as many as 3,000 foreign soldiers
assembled in Moscow at the beginning of this decade. Later
this massive body was divided and dispersed throughout
Russia. But its officers remained in Moscow, laying the foundation for a "new" foreign community, the so-called
"officers" community, which soon launched upon endless
discord with the old "merchants" community. When in 1653
foreigners were forbidden to own estates, part of the officers
living in villages also had to assemble in Moscow. Finally,
at the beginning of the 1660s, an entirely new group of foreign
officers were summoned to reorganize the military, and these
were placed in charge of the reorganized regiments. From this
moment the preponderance of military men in the Foreign
Settlement became evident.

The census of 1665 showed the following composition
of the populace of the New Foreign Settlement (by households):

	Households
Foreign military men (colonels to ensigns)	142
Specialists in military affairs (cannons, guns)	4
Specialists at court (gold and silver workers, watchmakers, saddlers, tailors, painters)	20
Doctors and druggists	4
Translators	3
Foreign merchants	23
Attorneys for commercial men	1
Jews	1
Pastors	3
Unknown titles	3
Total	204

Only homeowners were counted. Tenants are not included in
this calculation. The total number of people living in the

settlement at this time must be computed at not less than 1,500 (in the 1660s one could assume about 500, and about 1,000 by mid-century).

XVI

THE IMPACT OF WESTERN FAITH AND LITERATURE ON RUSSIA

The predominant religion of the Foreign Settlement long had been Lutheran. Although Catholicism had prevailed among the foreign population of Russia until the second half of the sixteenth century, the populace of the first settlement on the Yauza already had become largely Lutheran. Catholicism was known and suspect in Moscow as the faith of the neighboring Polish-Lithuanian state. The Russian Church long had cultivated hatred of "Latinism" among its adherents. Experiences of the Time of Troubles could only strengthen this hostile attitude. Hence, the Russian government, while summoning foreigners from all quarters, attentively ensured that those of the Latin faith did not pass into the Russian state. When Catholics were discovered among the soldiers recruited in Europe by Leslie, the government swiftly sent them packing back across the border at public expense. Throughout the entire century Catholics were also unsuccessful, despite many attempts, in securing permission to have their own church in Moscow, something the Lutherans and the Reformed had long enjoyed.

Conversely, the government treated Protestant religions very tolerantly, firstly, because there were no traditions or historical precedents connected with them and, secondly, because Protestantism was so alien to Orthodoxy that it seemed

heretical, not merely schismatic, and therefore impressed the
Russian government as less dangerous to the populace. Only
toward the end of the century did a small Catholic circle
form about Patrick Gordon[1] in the Foreign Settlement. But
it was unable to alter the general tone of religious life in
the settlement. Peter the Great, a student of the Foreign
Settlement, derived from the Settlement views that were Protestant.

Despite their relocation to the new settlement, foreigners
retained one legal entrance into the midst of their Russian
neighbors. This was by accepting Orthodoxy, something that
often occurred and was even voluntarily accepted when
foreigners married Russians. In olden times, during the sixteenth century, the Russification of foreigners had taken
place so gradually that the transition often proceeded as if of
its own accord. A man simply began to attend a Russian
church and to comply with Russian rites. An Orthodox priest
then baptized his children; and the second generation grew
up so Russified that it hardly remembered its foreign origins
and the nationality of its father. Only after the Time of
Troubles did the government intensify control over foreigners,
and a local Muscovite council in 1620 decreed that they
(that is, Catholics, for the question was not raised in regard
to Protestants) were to be baptized anew, like heretics. Then
the government turned against these semi-foreigners, whose
fathers had come to Russia at the time of Ivan the Terrible or
even Vasily III, and forced them to be rebaptized in their
old age.

The decree of the council of 1620, it is true, was repealed
by the council of 1667. Even then Russification possibly
occurred in the provinces as before, through a gradual blending, but this now became difficult in the capital. In Moscow
such an action would have been unprofitable as well, for
foreigners who resolved to accept Orthodoxy usually attempted
to derive from this transformation something more of profit.
They chose for themselves godfathers who were somewhat

more distinguished and a bit richer and beleaguered the government with petitions concerning their needs. They requested
and received money and estates and salaried positions and even
rewards in kind: clothing, food and drink and various household goods.

Formal conversion to Orthodoxy did not at all quicken
the process of Russification. On the contrary, individuals
who used to vanish into the Russian population actually had
been assimilated more quickly than was now the case, when
the "baptized" were surrounded by fellow countrymen who
encouraged their consciousness of national and cultural
exclusiveness. Now entire settlements in Moscow were populated by the "baptized." One such settlement formed a
geographical passageway from the Foreign Settlement to Moscow (this was Basmannaia; another, Panskaia, was located
on the other side of town). Thus the "baptized" also became
conductors of western influence to their Russian surroundings.

Less popular, though still more serious than the personal
influence of foreigners, was the impact of foreign literature
upon the emerging Russian intelligentsia. The conductors of
this influence again were the inhabitants of the Foreign
Settlement, albeit only their more cultured fellows. During
the Time of Troubles a certain boyar, Feodor Golovin,
had confidentially told a Pole, Maszkiewicz, that Golovin's
brother "had a strong inclination toward languages, but
could not study them openly. For this reason he secretly
lodged one of the Germans residing in Moscow. He had also
discovered a Pole who knew the Latin language. Both of
them met him secretly, disguised in Russian dress, locked
themselves in a room with him and together read Latin and
German books, which they had been able to acquire and
already understood rather well." Maszkiewicz himself saw
"a great many" of the books given to Golovin by his brother,
as well as attempts made by the highborn students to translate from Latin to Polish.

Little by little foreign books began to appear in the

provinces. In 1672 an interesting decree was promulgated by
which their dissemination was sternly forbidden: "In the
towns, in suburbs and settlements, in the districts, in villages
and in the countryside, in all places, people of all ranks are
to issue a firm order and reinforce it rigidly, that no one is to
keep printed Polish and Latin books secretly or openly in
his home but is to bring such books in and surrender them to
the governor." This order hardly proved efficacious. By
this same time a similar measure already was an anachronism
in the capital. As time passed domestic tutors and libraries
of foreign books became ever more common in Moscow, and
education itself was conducted more openly. In this manner
the famous Westernizers of the seventeenth century, Ordyn-
Nashchokin, [2] Matveev and Boris Golitsyn,[3] received their
education and educated their children.

In a letter to the Tsar written in 1671, the well-known
Ukrainian preacher and political figure, Lazar Baranovich,[4]
observed that "the council of His Royal and Most Radiant
Majesty does not disdain the Polish language, but reads Polish
books with delight." That this was not merely a compliment
directed toward the Muscovite boyars is demonstrated by
an attempt in 1672 by the printing house of a Kievan monastery to open in Moscow a special bookstore in which Polish
books would occupy a prominent place. Hitherto books had
been sold in Moscow from an official shop attached to the
Printing Office.[5] Open sale of books was conducted side by
side with other goods in the shops of Ovoshchny Riad. Yet
this attempt by the Kievans to open a special bookstore ended
unsuccessfully. On the one hand, it threatened to compete
with official and open sales in Moscow and, on the other, it
elicited fears that publications on theology and divine worship
suspect in Muscovite eyes would be disseminated from West
Russian and South Russian presses. A censor was appointed
(the manager of the Muscovite Printing Office, as it happened),
Metropolitan Paul, who discharged his duty in manner most
simple. Paul compared the Kievan books to earlier Muscovite

editions and noted their contradictions. Other books were
divided into two categories: books that had been offered for
sale in Moscow earlier and "concerning which there was no
controversy," and new books that were yet unknown in Moscow. The sale of "dissimilar" and unknown books was
then forbidden, because the selling of books that already
existed in Moscow offered them competition.

In the end it was natural that the government should
decide in 1675 that "no books should be sent to Moscow for
sale, because the Printing Office has been commissioned
to do this in Moscow, and there is *an abundance of books.*"
Yet Moscow's "abundance" seemed to apply only to books
intended for divine worship, which the official Printing
Office published almost exclusively. Inasmuch as the bookstore could carry only books of this sort, its Ukrainian
owners had to abandon their attempt to establish a special
book trade in Moscow.

This event did not erase the need for books of some sort.
It is interesting that the censor mentioned above had approved
for sale Latin and Polish books imported in 1672 by the
agents of a Kievan monastery. Russian traditionalists, however,
felt differently about these books. Representatives of this
Grecophile party (such as Evfimy)[6] had directly accused the
Russian aristocracy of fostering a vogue of Latin (that is,
unorthodox) ideas through their household tutors. When the
Academy[7] was being founded, this party also wished to
limit the incursion of western literature by introducing rigid
supervision of teachers of foreign languages and through
an unconditional prohibition against foreign books owned by
those who had not passed a course in higher learning. The
very conventionality of such ideas (irrespective of their total
impotence in practice) illustrates that restriction of literature by this means was now too late and could not succeed.

Foreign influence of this nature went farther than the
simple importing and reading of works from abroad. Foreign
libraries and teachers were really accessible to the aristocracy

alone. But with the flight of time foreign literature and
learning became increasingly popularized through Russian
translations. True, the vast majority of such translations
existed in a single copy that bore the autograph of the translator. In addition, many of these manuscripts were the
property of government institutions or were part of the
library of notable individuals. But a start was made. It is
possible to compile, however imperfectly, an instructive
set of statistics for these earliest Russian translations, which
were partly determined by the taste and needs of contemporary readers. The following table designates the number
of translations (known today) completed during three
fifty-year periods, from the sixteenth to the seventeenth
century, distributed according to branches of knowledge:

| | Number of translations | | |
Category	1550-59	1600-49	1650-99
Religious and moral	3	6	28
Literary	1	2	12
Historical	3	1	14
Cosmography and geography	4	1	7
Medicine	1	2	5
Encyclopedias, dictionaries and reference books	1	4	3
Astronomy	—	—	9
Military science	—	3	2
Natural science	3	1	—
Mathematics	—	—	3
Juridical and political	—	1	5
Various	—	—	6
Totals	16	21	94

However diverse the paths and forms of foreign influence,
however the force of this influence grew by the end of the
seventeenth century, its victory was still in the future, the work
of the next period of development of Russian national

consciousness. During the period under examination here, as
noted above, the critical spirit produced not the destruction
of nationalistic ideologies but, quite the contrary, their more
precise and complete formulation, It is necessary to pause
over this negative influence of western trends before passing
on to positive considerations. Above all, the reaction of
native nationalism to western influence must be analyzed.

XVII

NATIONALIST REACTION TO WESTERN INFLUENCE

Russian nationalistic reaction was at first unconscious, very
forceful in its manifestations but quite weak in its ultimate
results, for it originated among social strata having little influence. By the end of the century, however, this reaction
grew ever more systematic and conscious and converted
more influential groups of society. This reaction prospered
to the extent that it portrayed the degree and dimensions
of the danger with which nationalistic tradition was threatened by the spirit of criticism. If the nationalistic reaction
ultimately proved to be powerless despite its coherent nature,
its consciousness and its influential support, this was partly
because it realized too late the danger threatening nationalism,
partly because it could offer nothing as an alternative to this
danger, nothing with which to combat it. In Western Europe
these factors were absent and the nationalistic reaction
usually was better prepared if not to triumph over the critical
spirit at least to oppose it with stronger and more prolonged
resistance, thereby postponing the moment of its victory. In
Russia the resistance mounted by nationalism was paltry.

For this reason the triumph of critical tendencies usually was swift and complete.

A spontaneous, tribal hatred of foreigners is one of the elementary social feelings that accompanies national development as it proceeds from its lowest stages to the highest. This feeling is expressed weakly only where consciousness of national exclusiveness is weakly developed in general. Paul Dérouléde,[1] who vainly preached national hostility to the Russian peasant in the name of Leo Tolstoi, is the most graphic illustration of the two levels (we might say, two poles) of development of national consciousness. Expressions of national hostility are softened only in the highest stages of culture, under the influence of increased international relations and the achievement of universal unity and equality. But the thinness and fragility of this cultural layer of cosmopolitan ideas and sentiments are illustrated by the not infrequent outbursts of chauvinism and xenophobia among the cultured countries of the European West.

Before the end of the seventeenth century the national self-consciousness of the Russian people apparently was comparable to that of Tolstoi's peasant, that is, primitive indifference. It is erroneous, of course, to mistake that indifference for philosophical tolerance, inasmuch as its sole foundation was the total absence of impressions that arouse national irritation. But this state of affairs changed when such impressions began to accumulate and ceased to be accidental and isolated. The Time of Troubles was such an era. Incessant acts of violence against the habits and forms of the national way of life fostered and aggravated enmity among the residents of Moscow, while the plundering by Polish gangs throughout all Russia stimulated similar popularized feeling in the provinces. From the bewilderment caused by the actions of the First Pretender, Moscow quickly passed to the most passionate hatred. The rapidity of this change in attitude is seen, for example, in the case of the Greek bishop, Arseny of Thessaly,[2] a man of great craft. At the beginning of the

Troubles he supported the opinion voiced by Muscovite oppor-
tunists, that the Time of Troubles could be ended through
the marriage of Vasily Shuisky and Marina, the widow of the
Pretender.[3] But after enduring the difficult siege with the
Poles who were trapped in Moscow, Arseny finally considered
it convenient and opportune to bruit it about everywhere
that the liberation of Moscow from the Poles had been foretold to him in a dream by the national patron saint, Saint
Sergei.

From the moment that Moscow was liberated and
cleansed of Poles, ceremoniously the city preserved its hatred
of "paganism" as something sacred. In vain did the Protestant community in Moscow sing at the conclusion of its
divine services, instead of a religious hymn, the elegaic
"lament" composed by Pastor Baer[4] in 1610:

> O God, spread Thy cloak
> Over us in these days of sorrow,
> That because of our insidious enemies
> We shall not perish in the end.
> With all their heart and soul
> They dream of destroying us without trace
> From our native land.
> In no way can we reach an agreement.
> They say this and that,
> Yet we, the lowly, remain
> Fools in the end.
> However much you try, however you labor,
> Even if you bend backwards for them,
> Nothing ever pleases them.
> Wherever you cast your gaze,
> Your glance encounters only an enemy.
> The Tsar himself, and his entire royal court,
> Simply detest us.
> The common people cannot bear us.
> Whoever is not one of them is immediately

Given short shrift.

. . . .
From their bloodstained hands,
O God, deliver us!
Do not delay, appear suddenly,
And lead us from this place.
Be Thou our true Refuge.
Among these plains that mock us
Create a land for the Germans.
Thy flock lacks the strength
To live here longer, for new torments.
This barbarous Moloch is heavy for us,
We now must confess.
Lead us away or, heeding our supplication,
Call the unfortunate to Yourself,
To the Halls of Heaven.

The bitter moment passed and the scattered community was
almost reassembled, little by little. But the hostility of the
Russian populace had not changed. On the contrary, it intensified as the community grew in number and tried to draw
closer to the inhabitants of the capital. Always this enmity
was expressed in the most unambiguous manner. Street
urchins and adults sent the vilest curses after the foreigners,
just as recently heard and seen in the back streets of Istanbul.[5]
The foreigner who peeped into a church was thrown out,
and the floor was swept after him. Olearius[6] has recounted
several more serious incidents, which probably were not the
sole examples of this nature. Several passersby were walking
past the shop of a barber and noticed that in his quarters a
human skeleton was hanging. It seemed to them that this
skeleton moved whenever the barber played on a lute. Despite influential patrons, the ill-fated barber was banished from
Moscow. The skeleton was condemned to be solemnly burned.
In another case, a painter was barely rescued from reprisals
by the people when a skull was found in his home during a fire.

Because of such attitudes by the crowd, both Russians and foreigners had to observe the greatest prudence in their mutual dealings.

We observed earlier the boyar who wished to conceal a foreign teacher in his home by disguising him in Russian dress. By the middle of the century the situation had changed little, as is witnessed by the observations of Paul of Aleppo.[7] According to his account, Muscovites "regard someone of another faith to be extremely unclean. No Russian dares enter the dwelling of any of the Frankish (European) merchants to buy something from him but must go to his shop in the market. Even then he might be seized and told: You have gone there to become a Frank."

At the end of Michael's reign in 1643 the Muscovite clergy was already the instrument for venting irritation with foreigners. The clergy formally complained to the Tsar that foreigners erect their churches close to Russian churches and that they "keep Russian slaves in their courts, and these Russian slaves suffer every sort of sacrilege from these foreigners." This petition served as the signal for the government's persecution of foreigners discussed above. Immediately two Protestant churches were demolished, one in Pokrovka, the other near Chistye Prudy. Later the same fate befell a third. Then followed a series of decrees forbidding the wearing of Russian dress and the keeping of Orthodox domestics by foreigners, punishment of foreigners with death for blasphemy, the expulsion of English merchants from all the towns of Russia except Archangel and, finally, the eviction of all foreigners in 1652 from town limits to a settlement newly created for them.

These measures not only failed to extinguish national hostility toward foreigners but encouraged rowdies for the first time. The New Foreign Settlement was not yet completely built when street mobs attempted to sack it. Troubled by rumors that the wife of General Leslie (who had just been awarded a service estate) was torturing peasants and burning icons, the mob threw itself upon the New Foreign Settlement, destroyed the roofs of churches newly relocated there and demolished their preacher's pulpits and altars. Thereafter a special decree also forbade foreign ownership of service estates. Together these mandates forced foreigners into the isolated position mentioned earlier which, while more peaceful, actually posed a greater danger to Russian nationalism. Foreigners correctly likened their situation to that of a crab that someone decides to punish by drowning it in water.

Driving the foreigners from Moscow without first learning how to manage without their help really meant that foreigners now had to be approached in their own surroundings, in their own milieu, to gain the knowledge they possessed. The necessity to do so was not long in becoming apparent. Having deprived the foreigners of Russian domestics, the Russian government hesitated not at all in sending Russian children to a foreign school when theatrical performances at court demanded it. So it was that the children of lower commercial circles pointed out the way to be followed by the Tsar's own son.

XVIII

**YURY KRIZHANICH AND THE RUSSIAN
NATIONALIST TRADITION**

At this time hardly any Russian understood the impossibility of vanquishing European influences solely and purely by negative measures. The first to grasp the danger of impending Europeanization while refusing to limit his remedies to merely palliative measures was destined to be not a Russian, but a Croatian Slav, Yury Krizhanich (1617-1683). He

believed that the Slavs lived in such conditions that the danger
of foreign enslavement was incomparably great. Obvious
cases of such enslavement existed in the most diverse stages
and periods of Slavic history, beginning with economic
dependence, continuing on to cultural dependence and cul-
minating in political dependence. A perspective of this
nature afforded the beholder extraordinary vision.

Scholars have argued whether Krizhanich came to Russia
in the capacity of a Slavic patriot or as an agent of Catholic
propaganda sent to plead for the reunion of the churches. His
biography provides a clear answer to this controversy. As
a young man of 22 he had completed his training in Rome for
missionary work, having studied at Zagreb, Graz and Bologna.
In 1641 Krizhanich forwarded to the Congregation for the
Propagation of the Faith a report in which he unfolded a plan
to go to the schismatic brethren in Russia, "not so much
to preach the faith, as to summon them to virtue." Russians
"were also Christians, though in error." But they were also
"poor, pitiful simpletons and ignoramuses." He expected to
achieve his goals by approaching the "Grand Prince" and
convincing him that "in the entire Slavic world there is no sovereign more powerful than he." He intended to present himself as a translator and a tutor for the "prince's" children, then
to write a number of books and to persuade the grand prince
to liberate the Slavs and Europe from the Turks.

The Congregation concluded that Krizhanich was *o cervello
torbido e stravagante* (a confused and eccentric mind). They
buried him away not in Moscow, but in Varazdin (1642-1646).
Only through private efforts was Krizhanich able to relocate
to Smolensk and to reach his desired Moscow at the end of
1647, after a two-month journey as part of a Polish embassy.
Krizhanich later returned to Rome after a sojourn in Vienna
and a trip to Constantinople, then passed seven years in Rome,
waiting permission to leave for Russia. He finally received
this permission in 1657, only to have the Pope notice the pro-
nouncement made earlier by the Congregation. Thereupon

Krizhanich secretly left Rome and by his own efforts reached Moscow in 1658. In Moscow he displayed his tireless activity. He composed works and memoranda to the Tsar, offered to compile a grammar and lexicon of the Slavic language, corrected and published a Slavic Bible, composed a catalogue for the Tsar's library and translated books on history and political science. He offered his advice on how to appease the Ukrainian Cossacks[1] and labored, as the Tsar's historiographer, to refute "lies" being spread concerning Russia.

All these concerns and anxieties, however, met a reception in Moscow that was different from what this Slavic enthusiast had expected. He was distrusted as an alien and restive individual and was suspected of being a Catholic. His refusal to be baptized again, which was demanded for conversion to Orthodoxy, served as final evidence of his Catholic tendencies. In 1661 he was exiled from Moscow to Tobolsk, where he composed his "Politics," a resumé of his views which shall be examined below. Only after the death of Tsar Alexis did Krizhanich leave his exile and Russia. Once again he made his way among Catholics. In Vilna he entered the Dominican Order, a step apparently taken to facilitate his return to Rome. Receiving no support in this endeavor, he abandoned his monastic garb, departed Vilna without permission and, for this reason, found himself in a monastic prison. After serving a sentence of three months, he joined a new Slavic venture. Jan Sobieski was leaving to liberate Vienna from the Turks. Krizhanich joined his army and died beneath the walls of Vienna in 1683.

Such was the life of this celebrated Slav, who became the first theoretician of Russian national consciousness. Let us turn to an exposition of his thought.

XIX

KRIZHANICH'S DEFENSE OF SLAVIC CIVILIZATION

Even in the 1660s Russia struck Krizhanich as standing at the crossing of two cultural roads, one of which beckoned forward into a perilous future, while the other led backward into thick darkness. The outlooks of these two contradictory cultural orientations he formulated by drawing a great many striking comparisons. In each instance Krizhanich also indicated an escape from this dangerous dilemma, pointing to a middle path between the extremes of radicalism and reaction. This escape was dictated to him by "reason."

> There are two peoples seducing Russia with lures of a contradictory nature, drawing her and tearing her in opposite directions. These are the Germans and the Greeks. Although they are different in every respect, both agree as to the basic objective of their seductions.
>
> 1) The Germans recommend to us every sort of innovation. They wish us to forsake all our commendable ancient institutions and customs and to conform to their unnatural customs and laws. The Greeks, on the other hand, unconditionally condemn every innovation. Without reasoning further they howl and reiterate that every innovation is evil. *But reason says* that nothing is good or bad simply because it is new. Everything that now seems old once was new. One should not accept an innovation unthinkingly or frivolously, for one can err in

this. Yet the good must not be repudiated merely
because it is a novelty, for here error is also possible. In each case the matter must be seriously
examined before an innovation is accepted or rejected.

2) Once the Greeks taught us the Orthodox faith.
The Germans preach dishonest heresies that are fatal
to the soul. *Reason* here advises us that we should
be extremely grateful to the Greeks but should shun
and hate the Germans, for they are devils and dragons.

3) The Germans try to convert us to their school.
Under the guise of learning they palm off upon us
diabolical sorcery: astrology, alchemy and magic.
They advise us to open free knowledge (that is, philosophical knowledge) to general use and to make
knowledge accessible to every peasant. The Greeks,
on the other hand, condemn all knowledge and
all learning and recommend ignorance. *But reason
says:* avoid diabolical sorcery like the devil himself,
yet realize that ignorance, too, leads to no good.
As concerns philosophy and its study, it is pointless
to make such a fuss and to take such liberty as do
the Germans. One must imitate the modesty with
which the Holy Fathers studied and taught philosophy.
Just as every good taken to excess becomes evil, so
philosophy that is proclaimed to all men raises many
doubts and disturbances and distracts many from
work to idleness, as we see happening now among the
Germans. In Germany everyone without distinction,
the learned and the unlearned, honest and dishonest,
uses the common good for good or bad purposes—
one to find truth, another to prove his false opinion,
a third to justify vices. If every dish is flavored with
honey, sickness follows. So, too, philosophy ought
not to be made accessible to the people, but only
to the noble class and a few common people specially

designated, to the extent that they need it for government service. Otherwise something most worthy is profaned and grows commonplace, a pearl cast before swine.

4) The Germans regard preaching or reading the Gospel more important than everything else. Through this alone they hope to be saved, without penance or good works. They challenge us to public debates on this point. The Greeks, however, have abolished preaching and censure it. *But reason* advises us, first, to be jealous of penance and good works but, secondly, not to reject preaching. One should not entrust preaching to the first comer, who might be a priest or monk inexperienced or slack in his moral code. Preaching should be done only by the bishop or the oldest monks who are most experienced in life and who have said their last farewells to the temptations of the world. Simple clerics should be content with reading sermons from a book. And even this should not be permitted everyone, for in Germany and Poland any drunken priest can preach the word of God.

5) The Germans advise us to surrender to all corporal licentiousness and to disdain the practice of the monastic life, fasts, night vigils and all mortification of the flesh. The Greeks demand not only that we observe true and commendable Christian temperance but also that we adopt special types of false piety and hypocritical superstition. They wish to wash away spiritual blemishes with physical ablutions and hope to cleanse the uncleanness of the body through priestly prayers, and so on. *But reason* suggests that we not tolerate corporal licentiousness in any form and not neglect matters of fasting and the mortification of the flesh. New and suspicious forms of piety unknown to the Fathers should first be thoroughly examined.

6) In matters of politics the Greeks always exhort us to act according to the example of the Turkish Court. Unlearned and inexperienced on this question themselves, they tell us and can tell us nothing concerning this subject except what they see at the Turkish Porte. But the Germans censure all Turkish customs, laws and institutions. Everything bearing the name Turkish they *ipso facto* deem barbaric and inhumanly beastly. *But reason* says that even the Turks have some excellent institutions that are worthy of imitation, although not all of them are so.

7) The Germans assert that in matters of faith no one should be judged and cite Scripture on this point, where it is said: "Judge not, if you would not be judged." But the Greeks cite a different text: "Whoever preaches to us anything above that which has been received, let him be anathema." From this and similar passages they conclude that we must listen to them alone and believe them without argument. *But reason* advises us to reject without further consideration the German heresies and all other heresies already condemned by the Fathers and the councils. Should there arise any new controversial question that the Fathers and the councils have not examined and resolved, then listen first and investigate properly, condemning nothing without analysis (for example, questions concerning the number of sacraments and purgatory).

8) The Greeks fawn upon us and flatter us with fables, trying to extol the antiquity of our state while really defaming it and placing it in a disadvantageous position. They have called Moscow the Third Rome and have invented the humorous tale that the Russian realm is Roman, that the symbols of the dignity of the Roman Empire have passed to

it. The Germans, however, slander us and in every
possible way try to prove to the world that the
Russian state is simply a principality and that its
sovereigns are grand princes. Both deny our present
state its title and honor as a "kingdom" (*regnum*).
Both agree in their false interpretations that the Roman state was more than a kingdom and was something higher, that our present state cannot be compared to it in dignity, unless we have received such
dignity from the Romans. *But reason* says that only
God can appoint sovereigns, not the Roman Emperor.
To grant someone a crown and a title does not mean
that he thereby made a sovereign but simply that
one yields him one's own place. The Kingdom of
Russia is just as great and renowned as was Rome,
to which it never submitted, and is its equal in power.

9) From the above it is clearly seen how the Germans and Greeks subject us to various pernicious
temptations, while offering us advice that is directly
contradictory. The facts of the matter are as follows: 1) the Germans wish to contaminate us
with their novelties, while the Greeks censure every
novelty and foist upon us their own absurdities
under the false name of antiquity. 2) One sows
heresy; the other, though it has taught us the true
faith, has mixed this faith with schism. 3) One
offers us a blend of true science and that which is
diabolical; the other extols ignorance and considers
all science heretical. 4) One nourishes the vain
hope of salvation through preaching alone; the other
scorns preaching and prefers absolute silence.
5) One, tolerating every sort of licentiousness in
life, summons us upon the broad and spacious path
to ruin; the other, inciting us to hypocritical superstition and sanctimony, thereby points out to us
a path even narrower than the narrow and true path

to salvation.   6) One deems the entire Turkish state
system barbaric, tyrannical and inhuman; the other
finds it completely excellent and admirable.   7) One
considers it unlawful to judge anyone; the other as-
serts that the disobedient must be judged.   8) One
does no render the Russian state its true honor; the
other attributes to it honor that is fictitious, absurd
and impossible.   9) Although they differ almost in
all ways, they agree perfectly in their mutual detesta-
tion of our people and hold us in contempt, speak
scandal about us and heap upon us the bitterest cal-
umnies and blame.

This long citation does more than summarize the author's
views on the question at issue here; it also poses this question
fully. The contest between Greek and German cultural influences could be treated in this manner only by a man who
was foreign to both, who looked upon Protestantism and
Orthodoxy through the eyes of a Catholic and who hated the
Greeks and the Germans as a Balkan Slav, a Slav from that
border region where the arrogant domination of the Greek ad-
joined the enterprising exploitation of the German. Krizhanich also understood well that only past traditions supported
the Greek, who would lose ground before a Slavic revival.
But the future belonged to the German, who could be opposed
only with his own weapon, the development of native culture.
For this reason, and not merely because it was rather unwise
to attack the Greeks in Orthodox Moscow, all of Krizhanich's
efforts naturally were directed toward the struggle, not with
the Greeks, but with those who were, to his mind, the main
enemy of the Slavs, the Germans. The strength of Krizhanich's
hatred for this enemy was equalled only by the involuntary
respect with which he was filled for European culture.

XX

KRIZHANICH ON THE DANGER OF FOREIGNERS IN RUSSIA

This theoretician of nationalism entered upon his literary struggle with equipment that was markedly different from that possessed by the immature foes of foreign influence. Accordingly, his publicistic preaching displays two very disparate sides. When he curses the Russian love for foreigners, we can imagine the satisfaction with which the most inveterate Muscovite Old Believers followed the thrust of his speeches. But once he passes on to the means of healing this bitter illness, it is also easy to imagine how their faces fell. Peter the Great himself spoke like a Slavic patriot when he addressed these people.

"People who are gifted and wise usually exploit other, less cultured people (*populos rudiores*)." Here is Krizhanich's point of departure. "In former times the Greeks lured other peoples into deception; now the Germans seduce them." The main reason for this is the weakness of native cultural development. "Our people occupy a middle ground between wild and civilized peoples." Slavs suffer in comparison with civilized peoples. "We are mediocre in appearance, while foreigners are beautiful and therefore arrogant and proud. We are taciturn; they are glib of tongue, loquacious and full of mocking, abusive and caustic discourses. We are slow of mind and simple of heart, while they are filled with ruses of every kind. We are idlers and wasters and do not keep account of our incomes and expenditures; we give away and throw away our wealth. But they are miserly, greedy and wholly devoted to profit. Day and night they watch to see how they might fill their pockets, then laugh at our banquets and entertainments. We are lazy in our work and toward the sciences, while they are industrious and do not sleep away a single opportune hour. We are content with miserable clothing and a frugal way of life. They are demanding and roll in luxury and delight, never sated by anything, continually hungering and desiring more and more. We live in a miserable land; they were born in rich and luxurious countries and bring us goods for luxury and enjoyment, such as pearls, silk, precious stones, wine, sugar and fruits. With these enticements they trick us, as hunters do beasts. We speak and think simply and act simply in all we do; if we quarrel, we make peace again. But they have hearts that are secretive, insincere and rancorous, with affected exteriors. They cannot forget an offensive word until death; and if they quarrel with you once, true peace cannot be made for centuries. Even after reconciliation always they seek the occasion for revenge."

The advantages enjoyed by foreigners blind us and deliver us into their hands. "With a tongue most imperfect, almost mute, with our weakness of mind and almost total lack of beauty, we see marvelous eloquence, wisdom, intelligence and art in games and flattering jokes. Like birds that more easily fall into the hunter's snare the more they become curious and marvel at the hunter's work, we gape at foreign beauty, often are made fools of by foreigners, and are driven mad. Foreigners throw a bridle upon us, mount our backs and ride us wherever they wish." Having fascinated us with their beauty and deceived us by their intelligence and cunning, foreigners then "exact tribute from us, fleece us and drive us to destitution thanks to our cupidity and greed. They beat us, injure us and expose us to the ridicule of all peoples with their devilish arrogance."

But have the Slavs really been destined to remain the eternal juveniles in the family of civilized men? Can this relationship between them and the foreigners be altered? According

to the sense of Krizhanich's thought, some part of this relationship cannot be altered, some of it should not be altered, but
some parts of it deserve to be changed. This relationship *cannot*
be altered if the national characteristics here portrayed are
considered inherent, innate traits of national character. Krizhanich is inclined to regard in this category several of the
national traits just mentioned. "Taciturnity, laziness, carousing
and wastefulness," he says, "are really our birthmarks, four
primordial characteristics with which we seem to have been
born." But along with these natural defects he also mentions
natural virtues that *must not* be altered. "The first of the good
fortunes that are ours by birth is that seemingly we are not
ambitious . . . and are content with a simple way of life."

Ignoring immutable national peculiarities, Krizhanich re-
duces the remaining differences between Slavs and foreigners
apparently to a single factor: the *level of knowledge and
skill*. Ignorance is a flaw inevitably cured by time. "Every
man is born simple and unskilled in all things. Slowly he grows
in body; even more slowly is his reason perfected. Only at
age fourteen or later do countless people look around themselves and begin to understand the world and what is happening
in it . . . . Not only individuals but whole peoples learn slowly
and slowly are perfected in reason. Much time must pass before
peoples come to know the truth and to abandon ancient, bad
(that is, harmful) ideas and laws. Only then do they learn to
make suitable what was unsuitable, to reduce the inopportune
to the convenient, to change the good to something even
better, to transform the vile into something decent and honorable . . . . The Roman historian, Florus, properly has likened
the history of his people to the four ages of man (childhood,
youth, maturity and old age) . . . . With good reason we can
apply this division of ages to every other people. This shows
that not only are all human things inconstant and changeable
but also that every people does not perceive the rationality and
wisdom required for its social life and governmental organization immediately or in a single moment, but after much time
has passed."

"Just as bravery is passed on from people to people, so is wisdom. In ancient times some peoples, such as the Egyptians, Greeks and Jews, were acquainted with all sciences, yet now are ignorant. Others were coarse and wild during ancient times, but now are splendidly renowned in the professions and in wisdom of all sort, as are the Germans and the French . . . . Let no one say that the path to the sciences apparently is forbidden to us Slavs by some sort of divine destiny and that seemingly we cannot or should not study the sciences. Just as other peoples have learned from each other, gradually and not in a single day or a single year, we can also school ourselves, if we wish and if we try."

Not all Slavs, however, find themselves in circumstances sufficiently auspicious for acquiring the sciences. Krizhanich notes the vanity of suggesting a Slavic Renaissance in Pomerania, Silesia, among the Czechs or in Moravia, for these lands already are Germanized. The Slavs beyond the Danube (Bulgars, Serbs and Croats) also "have long ago lost not only their states but all their strength, their language and their reason as well . . . . To help them fully and to restore their states in these difficult times is impossible. Only books can open the intellectual eyes of such people; then they can learn to understand their own dignity and begin to consider their own regeneration." Awakening national consciousness among the Poles would be an easier task, but outside assistance is needed even for this.

Only the Muscovite sovereign can render such assistance to all Slavs. The eyes of all Slavs are upon him. He alone can gather the scattered flock and restore a human semblance to those reduced to an animal condition by foreign influence, as if by the wonder-working potion of Circe. Not in vain has God raised up in Russia a Slavic kingdom which, in power, glory and majesty, has seen no equal among Slavs. "The example of other peoples teaches that once a state reaches the pinnacle of power, the sciences begin to flourish among its people . . . . So it is rational to suppose that the time has finally come for our people, too, to learn the sciences."

But if Russia is to play such a role in the Slavic world, Russia itself must be cleansed of the sin of "foreign mania," the craze for things foreign to which even Russia has been exposed, though to a lesser extent than other Slavs. "Now is the time to drive the Germans away once and for all. It is loathsome to study for a lifetime without learning, remaining forever on the pupil's bench."

Through this philosophy of history Krizhanich arrives at a merciless analysis of Russia's "foreign mania." Once Krizhanich touches upon this theme, he spares no words, does not shrink from exaggeration, is undisturbed by radical conclusions, if only Russia can be saved from the mournful fate, based upon the precedents of other Slavs, he fancies to be visible in the near future. He thoroughly searches out vestiges of European influence in contemporary Russia, tries to detect their deleterious aspects and appeals for national convictions to replace those that are foreign. Not restricting himself to present borrowing, he depicts the dangers of future borrowing, cautions against it and defends against it the good, old customs still preserved in Russia.

The two basic foundations of state power are material wealth and military strength. In both respects Russian power is threatened by the invasion of foreigners. Their merchants suck out the wealth of the country. They know how to purchase Russian goods for next to nothing, while foisting their own goods upon Russians at enormous prices. Moreover, they import goods that merely serve to corrupt Russians even more by exposure to foreign influences and export goods that Russia absolutely needs for the further growth of its population (such as corn grain).

Hiring foreigners for military service does not increase Russia's military strength as much as it diminishes it. Before speaking of the hiring of entire corps, Krizhanich firmly expresses his opinion against the invitation of foreign officers that had been practiced on a broad scale during the 1630s and reached especially large proportions in the 1660s, just as

Krizhanich was writing his book. The "colonels" were not
teaching Russian troops what they needed. They introduced
the heavy formation, quite suitable for warfare on the western border but impractical for battle with the southern nomads
who posed to Russia a particular peril. Russians could have
taught themselves how to shoot arquebuses and bear long lances.
Having introduced these reforms in the infantry Russians also
erred by adopting the German mounted formation, instead of
retaining the "light riding and hussars' formation" proven by experience. At the same time inviting foreigners to fill the highest positions in the military closed the way to Russians, who
lost all hope of winning promotion, then lost even the desire to
serve. The common soldiers who obeyed the commands of
a foreigner lost confidence in themselves and their superiority
over other peoples, even while they failed to gain faith in
their new commanders.

How can this situation be resolved? Here Krizhanich
favors radical measures. Foreign merchants and the colonels
must be driven from the Russian land. The former should
be retained only until they have transmitted their skills to the
Russian people. And they should be awarded nothing beyond
what they have already given Russia.

Krizhanich then goes further. From present dangers he
passes to dangers that threaten in the future. Between the
two stages lie what has been borrowed already from foreigners
in all areas of life. Krizhanich amusingly postulates the in-
significance of such borrowings and sketches the complete and
enduring contrast existing between the European and the
Russian way of life. This contrast accounts for most of the accusations and jibes by foreigners. Krizhanich readily admits
that not all these accusations are false. But he always answers
the foreigners with passionate reproaches that verge upon
the opposite extreme. As always, he posits the golden mean as
the objective to be sought. It is true, of course, that Russian
dwellings are extremely uncomfortable, that the windows are
narrow, the vents for passing smoke are small and that when

heating on a rainy day smoke remains in the hut and blinds the
eyes. It is true that there is eternal dirt beneath the benches
in the hut, that dishes remain unwashed and that breathing is
impossible because of the stench. But the homes of foreigners
tend toward effeminacy. Their marble floors are washed so
often and are maintained in such cleanliness that they resemble
altars. A guest cannot spit on the floor without a housemaid
immediately wiping it up. "We should not imitate the cleanliness of the foreigners, which is too meticulous and spares no
labor," these foreigners who wish to transform our temporary,
earthly inn into the palaces of Heaven. A home must be clean.
Its utensils must be suited to washing and not be caulked or
carved. The furniture should be of native wood, not of imported material.

The same is true of dress. It is true that the Russian costume fails to satisfy a single basic requirement for clothing.
It is uncomfortable, flimsy, expensive and heavy, with a cut
that disfigures a man and is homely to boot. In addition, a
Russian has to conceal his handkerchief in his hat, his money
in his mouth and his knives, papers and all else that he needs
in his boots. All this prompts the gibes and aversion of
foreigners. The shortcomings of our fashions must be offset
by the wealth and brightness of our material and expensive
trimmings: furs and precious stones. No one can disclaim the
sensibleness and practicality of European fashion. But Europeans have a new style each year. There are no adornments or
fashions to enhance comfort or mood that they do not in-
vent. "France or any other country finds it worthwhile to de-
vise something savory, playful, frivolous or luxurious, for
the Germans immediately come running and zealously adopt
it." Russians should create a style that is a mean between that
of the East and the West. It should be cheap, comfortable
for movement, simple and light.

Krizhanich unconditionally prefers the Russian way of
life to that of the Europeans. Europeans "consider enjoyment
the highest pursuit of man" and maintain that "man was

created by God to make use of earthly pleasures." In so doing
"they change Christ's Gospel into a gospel of enjoyment."
They regard our simplicity of life as barbarism. The Russian,
after a good night's sleep taken haphazardly upon a bench
or on the stove, covered with his own clothing instead of a quilt,
on straw bedding instead of a mattress, very early rushes off
to work or to serve the Tsar. The foreigner pampers himself until midday on featherbeds, then, after he has hardly risen from
his bed, sits down to a tasty breakfast. He devotes his time to
idleness, varying his leisure with games, songs, music, dances
and delighting his taste through a thousand dishes with every
possible flavoring. Yet while the upper class ("men like Sarda-
napalus" or "loungers") roll in luxury, the landless workers
are steeped in destitution. "For a whole year they drink nothing
but clear water and live on insufficient bread alone." "But in
Russia all people, by the kindness of God, the richest as well as
the poorest, eat rye bread, fish and meat and drink kvas, even
if they lack beer." They live in roofed huts, while in the West
the poor endure winter in the cold, "for houses are sold by
weight." "Thus the life of the peasant and farm worker is far
better in Russia than in many countries."

Krizhanich sees the most important advantage of the Russian social order in its insistence that all social groups engage
in service to society, with no one allowed to remain idle. In
Russia there are no unproductive social groups, or their number is held to a minimum. "The peasants till the soil and
bake bread. The military men suffer cold and hunger, shed
their blood and are considered chiefs. The aristocracy wage war,
judge law cases, think thoughts and serve their king through
advice and labor. Clerics and monks entreat God because of the
sins of the people. Under such a system all good and productive classes do nothing but serve the common good of all classes."
Krizhanich deliberately excludes from this list the merchants
and those whom we call the intelligentsia. To his mind the merchants, like idle segments of the aristocracy, are an unproductive, "mercenary" class of "do-nothings." The intelligentsia,

except for a minimum few, struck him as parasites, causing more harm than good. There is no need whatsoever to encourage their teaching of liberal studies, which is too broad.

XXI

KRIZHANICH'S POLITICAL THOUGHT

In his political thinking Krizhanich expresses an attitude toward the Russian autocracy that is highly characteristic of him. Continually and persistently he repeats that absolute monarchy is one of the most vital foundations of national prosperity. In addition to the argument heard often today — that autocracy assures the freedom of every individual against the encroachments of influential persons and classes and defends the weak against the strong — Krizhanich states another reason that is especially important to him. The evil that he dislikes in Russia flows for the most part, or so he thinks, from *lack of knowledge*; that is, it is the fruit of simple errors that can be corrected through legislation. "Bad lawgiving" is the root of all evils. Consequently, radical legislative reform must be the basic medicine. The absolute power of the sovereign is, Krizhanich feels, a necessary condition for achieving such radical legislation. Hence, he defends this principle with special passion. But upon closer investigation Krizhanich's reasoning can be seen to follow his customary schema: Russia is one extreme; the Slavs are another. Truth lies in the mean.

"Our people do not know how to take certain measures in order to follow a middle course, but always proceed to extremes. Here we find a Slavic state system that is extremely undisciplined, willful and disorderly, and there we find one that is extremely

stable, firm and brutal. The entire world knows no kingdom
in such disarray and so dissolute as Poland. But nowhere
is there as stern a domain as in this glorious Russian state."
Foreigners and their influence prove to be responsible
for both extremes. "Foreigners have contaminated the world
with dissolution and limitation of autocracy." From foreigners the Poles copied their own anarchy. The individual
who began the "oppression of people" (tyranny) in Russia was
Ivan the Terrible. Ivan "wished to make himself a Varangian,
or a German, or a Roman or anyone but a Russian or a Slav."
Not satisfied with acquiring power in this manner, Ivan desired
vain glory. His "court braggards" (Krizhanich did not suspect
that some of them were Slavs and laid this blame upon Greeks,
particularly Patriarch Jeremiah, who visited Russia in 1588)
invented for him absurd and harmful fables of how Moscow
was the Third Rome and its sovereign a descendant of
Augustus. Such vanity was "not the least or the most insignificant reason for the ruin of Moscow and other national
calamities that the Russian people have suffered since Tsar
Ivan's time."

Returning to the "oppression of people," Krizhanich emphasized its detrimental effect upon domestic and foreign
policy. A stern regime is accompanied by extortions that en-
rich the royal treasury but bring the common people to
ruin on an incomparably large scale. These financial burdens
can cause the decline of a country. By the same token,
this sternness antagonizes neighbors. Thus the Ukrainians,
having experienced Muscovite overlordship, hastened to return
to Polish rule.

Krizhanich argued long and hard against both extremes,
the "oppression of people" and "dissolution." Rather than
dwell upon these polemics, it is more valuable to examine the
positive conception of the "moderate regime" that this
publicist developed as his own type of "enlightened absolutism."
His theory again was that golden mean to which his sympathies
invariably gravitated.

"Ask all the kings on earth how they understand their obligations, and you will discover that many of them cannot explain distinctly why God created kings upon the earth and why He gave them power over peoples. Kings imagine that they were not created for the sake of kingdoms and peoples, but that kingdoms were created for their sake. Kings imagine that their only business is to rule, to command, to enjoy pleasures and not to think night and day of the good of their people." Whatever the origin of power, in reality it is limited, either by the will of God (if perchance power was acquired from a prophet or by means of conquest) or by the will of the people (in elected monarchies the power of each sovereign is unique, while in hereditary monarchies it is the power of "the first, who is freely chosen from the people to reign," which practically amounts to the same thing). Thus, although "the king is subordinate to no human power and no one can judge him, he is subordinate to God's command and to public opinion (the common voice). These two chains bind the king and remind him of his duty. Whoever is untroubled by the fear of God, or the shame of men, or the glory of future ages is the true, absolute tyrant." Tyranny is as great a shame to a king as cowardice is to war, or infidelity to marriage, or falsehood to the nobleman, or theft to the rich man.

"The concern, obligation and main business of a king is that of *making his people blissful*." To this he must direct all his thoughts. But everything is not possible, of course, even for a Tsar. No Tsar can hope to guarantee that his reign is absolutely free of all shortcomings. He cannot force the earth to yield fruit or force the sea to produce fish. But it does not necessarily follow that the sovereign has the right to leave uncorrected what can be corrected. However full of good intentions, he must remember that he may be succeeded by someone of a different frame of mind. A more trustworthy means of securing betterment over a long period of time is provided by "good statutes." Good legislation, however, is

not achieved easily. One must "think much and weigh things,
search in books and trouble one's head. Amid other cares
the king and his advisers find it difficult to bear in mind so
many calculations and various considerations or to glean from
books graphic examples from earlier times." For all these
reasons and as an antidote to the false counsels of flatterers,
"the wise sovereign must keep by his side at least one or
two philosophers, having the rank of mentor or chronicler,
who will reveal to him the other side of truth or, should they
themselves fear to proclaim the truth, at least indicate books
that are unafraid to speak the truth."

Krizhanich obviously meant such a role for himself. His
desire was fulfilled, though in a rather peculiar manner. He
was sent into honorable exile with a large salary, an arrange-
ment that he formally approved and considered commendable
in his *Politics*. From distant Tobolsk he could submit his
political counsels without danger to the tranquility of the state
or to himself. For several successive years he worked at this
task. The product of these voluntary studies in involuntary
seclusion was his unique philosophy of nationalism, which
casts such bright light upon the aspirations of the times.

The counsels that Krizhanich offered were not confined
to criticism of the present; nor were they limited to negative advice concerning the closing of Russia to foreigners.
During his free time he elaborated and proposed to the government a whole series of positive reforms in all areas of
political and social life. According to his plan, the Tsar himself should inform his people of these reforms in a long
speech, which Krizhanich composed for him and which included a resume of all of Krizhanich's proposals. Analysis of all
these measures is unnecessary. But their mutual connections
must be studied in some detail, so that through these nationalistic longings the scope of Krizhanich's reformatory thought
might be determined.

XXII

KRIZHANICH'S SOCIAL AND ECONOMIC THEORIES

Perhaps it would not be erroneous to identify as the central idea of Krizhanich's program the need to develop Russia's productive forces. "The primary cause of state power is an overabundance of people," he observed. "People propagate and grow numerous where there is food, clothing and other things required for human existence, such as peace and a well organized government. Everywhere people breed according to how the land can support and feed them, that is, to the extent that the land and water yield bread, livestock, fish, animals for food and clothing, as well as villages, and stone and ore for fashioning dwellings, utensils and weapons. But where the land is barren the population must be sparse as well. It is true that in some places, Holland for example, there are many more people than the land can sustain, but these live through their great development of manufacturing and trade, and by importing food and clothing from abroad. On the other hand, there are places where the land is fertile but people are few. Plague, famine and war can account for this. But such situations do not long continue; the land is soon populated anew. If the land remains underpopulated for a half century or more, the causes must be different." Such causes might be the poor development of agriculture, handicrafts and commerce, coupled with economic exploitation of the country by foreigners, or bad laws and a stern tyranny (accompanied by heavy extortions). Measures to increase the density of population can be three-fold: first, by direct legislative decrees; secondly, by all procedures aimed at development of native manufacturing and commerce, with limitation of foreign competition; thirdly, changes in the system of government in conjunction with sound fiscal policies.

One direct legislative action toward the settlement of the country and the propagation of its populace is the facilitation and encouragement of marriages by all means possible. But nothing hinders this objective more than settling foreigners and registering them as citizens. The Roman Empire was ruined because it became more and more ethnically mixed as its conquests increased. The Russian state, however, is strong because of its national unity. Krizhanich sharply opposed the conversion of foreigners and the recruitment of entire corps of outsiders for state service.

Krizhanich offers a great many practical suggestions for the development of Russia's productive forces. As observed, the complete banishment of foreigners is the basis of his outlook. Because he is hostile to commercial middlemen, he regrets even the surrender of the profits of foreign trade to Russian private enterprisers. He would pass these profits entirely to the treasury, which would conduct all wholesale trade with foreigners. It is impossible to enumerate here all his separate counsels concerning searches for new sources of natural wealth, the organization of new manufacturing enterprises, the introduction of new instruments of production and processing of Russian raw materials, the opening of new trading stations, the adoption of European forms of credit, and the like.

As for sound financial policies, Krizhanich begins with criticism of tyrannical extortions that extract from the populace ten times more than the amount reaching the treasury. The basic principle that he "does not tire of repeating" serves as his rule: when the people are rich, the king also is rich. When the people are poor, the king is poor as well. He suggests that all government levies be replaced by a single, direct tax, the collection of which should be entrusted to local self-government.

There remains the delicate question of introducing certain

legal limitations to monarchical power. Krizhanich intended
to resolve this problem by assigning to various classes moderate privileges, or "temporary liberties." Far from limiting
autocracy, these "temporary liberties" would prove useful
only to the autocrat. "Among the French and the Spaniards
the magnates enjoy certain liberties in keeping with their
lineage; and in return the kings suffer no dishonor either
from the common people or from the army. But among the
Turks, where such liberties are not extended on the basis
of birth, the sovereigns are at the mercy of the stupidity and
insolence of common foot soldiers. The king must do whatever the Janissaries wish. The insolence of the taxed people
(these words Krizhanich places upon the lips of Tsar Alexis
Mikhailovich) is clearly evident among us and known to you.
All this insolence stems from the boyars' lack of the power
and strength needed to keep the taxed people in check and to
restrain them from violent actions. This is why we wish to
grant you, our servants, appropriate liberties." In this manner,
according to Krizhanich's thought, the "temporary liberties"
that he proposed would create a sort of *pouvoirs intermediares*,
spoken of by Montesquieu. These would transform the "oppression of people" into a "moderate regime" ("autocracy"
into "monarchy," to use the terminology of Catherine II and
Alexander I).

But class liberties must not limit autocracy. They are
conferred conditionally and can be revoked at any time. On
the other hand, they must not upset the basic principles
of Muscovite state practice, which Krizhanich unconditionally
approves, such as "closing the borders" (the ban against
travel abroad) and the rule that every man is registered to his
work and cannot remain idle. A single exception can be
made for "distinguished boyars;" after three successive years
of service at court or in the army, a boyar should be freed
until his death from court service and should not be obliged
to come to court or to live in Moscow, unless he is specially
summoned. According to Russian conceptions, of course, such
a summons would be tantamount to disgrace.

For the highest class, the "princes," a new law would be created—that they possess fortified towns. The middle service class would be exempt from corporal punishment and from confiscation of their property, except for crimes against the state. The sovereign would, nonetheless, retain the right to exile members of the middle service class without trial. Only the middle service class would enjoy the right of owning service estates. They would be given preference for training in higher education.

Commerce and manufacturing would enjoy freedom from interference by any state monopoly or privileged state enterprise. Handicraftsmen would be organized into guilds. Towns would receive self-government. Other liberties envisaged by Krizhanich would lead to abolition of the humiliating manner of approaching those in authority (such as beating one's head on the ground, calling the suppliant a slave, using diminutive names) and to the formulation of titles and outward signs of respect.

Frightened by precedents from the history of the West and South Slavs, Krizhanich was particularly fearful that "foreign mania" might become "foreign rule," that is, domination by a foreign dynasty that would lead finally to political enslavement. To avert this possibility he felt that a precise law should be drawn to regulate succession to the throne. The sovereign should bind the people with an oath that under no circumstances would they tolerate a foreigner on the throne. Should the dynasty end, the throne should be passed on to one of twelve "princes," who comprise the highest class of the state and who are granted this title by the sovereign.

When all these reformatory projects by this first theoretician of Russian nationalism are recalled, one enters the realm of ideas that led to the reforms of Peter and Catherine. Nationalism is synonymous with reform in Krizhanich's fundamental assertion: to combat a higher culture the sole necessary and effective means is the cultivation of the

independent development of the native culture. Strictly speaking, this notion is Catherine's, rather than Peter's. To Peter
independent activity was not yet a goal, but merely a result that
flowed naturally from the conditions of his time. Even when
Peter acted expediently and consciously, as he did in developing
Russia's productive forces, to him this development was a
means toward an immediate goal, the enlargement of state resources. To Krizhanich, a thinker schooled in politics, this
immediate, direct goal had lost utterly the autonomous meaning
it long enjoyed during the spontaneous process of Russian state
development. Systematically Krizhanich subordinated the
state to the task of serving national life. Moreover, even the
free play of national life served Krizhanich merely as a means
toward a still higher goal, the preservation of national unicity.

Without preservation of this uniqueness it was unthinkable that the final and most cherished goal of all the publicistic
work of this Slavic patriot and confirmed Catholic could be
realized: the goal of liberating the Slavs and uniting the
churches. It was partly the remoteness of his main objective
and partly his serious political schooling that gave Krizhanich
the insight that distinguishes his statement of this problem.
To find a similar conscious profession of the national question
by a true Russian publicist, we must skip an entire century
directly to Boltin,[1] that is, to the time of Catherine II.

In the interim very much of what Krizhanich had proposed
to Tsar Alexis was attained. But experienced also were many
of those things that had plunged Krizhanich into trembling and
horror when contemplated as the merest possibility. All the
externals of European culture were adopted without modification, quite mechanically, as Krizhanich had feared. Sweet
food, soft beds, the refined idleness of the upper class, the lux-
uriousness of furniture, dress and dwellings—all became commonplace. Russia even endured the "foreign rule" Krizhanich
dreaded most of all. A foreigner, who also happened to be a
woman, occupied the throne, a consequence of the absence of
the law on succession that Krizhanich had persistently called

to the attention of the government. In short, the entire course
of cultural life displayed no sign of the awareness Krizhanich
had demanded of it. Yet all of Krizhanich's fears proved completely unfounded. Russia was not denationalized; instead,
gradually it assimilated the elements of foreign culture once
grasped mechanically. Did this not mean that the perils stated
by Krizhanich were impossible for Russia?

Denationalization can occur only when and where sufficiently strong elements of national organization have not
been created, or where national reticence has yielded its place
to conscious cosmopolitanism. Russia had not produced
either condition. Russia had passed through the formless, ethnographic homogeneity that had allowed the total Germani-
zation of the Slavs inhabiting the eastern German marches. Yet
Russia had not attained the level of culture wherein cosmopolitanism might flourish. Having reached an intermediate stage
in its development, Russia proved invulnerable to foreign influences stronger even than those of modern times, thanks to its
low level of development and gigantic size. For this reason
the notion of denationalization could occur only to a foreign
observer who was familiar with what had happened elsewhere.

The ideas and sentiments that dictated Krizhanich's
misgivings were undoubtedly real enough. But Krizhanich
examined them in the magnifying glass of his personal political
and historical knowledge. Thus the dose of foreign poison
that life had injected (or was about to inject) into the Russian
organism struck him as being strong enough to produce a
fatal outcome. In reality, the living native body was sufficiently
healthy to find this infusion just powerful enough to act as a
healing inoculation.

NOTES

**CHAPTER I   THE RISE OF MOSCOW AND
MUSCOVITE IDEOLOGY**

1. Rus was the name given to the eastern Slavic state that came into existence during the ninth century along the river systems of what is today European Russia. This cohesive political formation was apparently administered from its capital at Kiev as a political and economic whole until the twelfth century, when Rus fell into civil war and was fragmented into a number of semi-independent principalities. After the Mongol invasion of the thirteenth century, many of these principalities transferred their allegiance to or were incorporated by Lithuania-Poland. The subsequent aspiration of the Muscovite grand prince to "gather the lands" of Rus under his control ran counter to the intentions of Rurikid princes who wished to preserve their autonomy within their principalities and often led to conflict with the Lithuanians and Poles, who also claimed the inheritance of Rus.

2.   Yarlyk was a term of Tatar origin that signified immunities or privileges granted by the Khan of the Golden Horde to Russian princes and ecclesiastics. Here Miliukov refers to the yarlyk, or charter, that the Khan bestowed upon the Russian prince designated to serve as grand prince.

3. Ivan I Kalita (1328-1341) was grand prince of Moscow and the Tatar agent for the collection of taxes throughout Russia. From the wealth that he accumulated from imposing tribute upon trade along the northern river systems and by diverting to his coffers part of the taxes gathered in the name of the Mongols, Ivan Kalita (whose nickname means "the Moneybag") was able to purchase neighboring principalities, ransom Russian prisoners and recruits from the Mongols and generally increase the economic and political might of Moscow.

4. In Muscovite times the term volost referred to administrative territorial divisions as well as peasant communities that comprised several rural peasant settlements.

5. Alexis (Aleksei) became Metropolitan of the Russian Church during the reign of Ivan Kalita. In 1357 he reconciled Prince Vsevolod of Kholm and Prince Vasily of Tver, thereby preventing civil strife and winning for himself a reputation for peace-making. Here Simeon attempts to impress upon all princes the obligation to submit their individual feuds and quarrels to the metropolitan for arbitration.

6. An appanage (*udel*) was a common term for princely land holdings inherited by one man after a patrimony had been divided among several heirs.

7. The Pani (singular, Pan) were members of the feudal aristocracy of Poland and Lithuania. Some Pani owned thousands of serfs and supplied their own military detachments in time of war. They also held key positions in national and regional government.

8. Ivan's father, Vasily II, was grand prince from 1425 to 1462. The first twenty-five years of his reign were marred by civil war over succession to the office of grand prince. During this struggle Vasily's opponents, led by the brother of Vasily I, blinded him. For this reason Vasily II is often termed "the Dark," or "the Blind."

9. Ivan was determined that his four brothers, who shared the inheritance of Vasily II, should regard themselves as his vassals and be limited in their power and wealth. After much discord, his two elder brothers, Boris and Andrei, unsuccessfully rebelled against him in 1480.

10. Following his consecration as metropolitan in Constantinople, Peter assumed the title of "Metropolitan of Kiev and All Rus." From his arrival in the principality of Vladimir in 1309, Peter had much to say concerning the policies of the grand prince, Mikhail Yaroslavich, and was also active in political matters that involved the Golden Horde.

11. Metropolitan Isidore had represented the Russian Church at the Council of Ferrara-Florence, which proclaimed the reunion of the Eastern and Latin Churches in 1439. Four years later the Russian Church repudiated the union of Florence and deposed Isidore from his office.

CHAPTER II   EUROPE DISCOVERS MUSCOVY

1. The survivors of the Byzantine royal family were, of course, potential successors to the throne of Constantinople, should the Turks be driven from Asia Minor. Many western political powers, considering the liberation of Byzantium still possible, were anxious to secure political rights to the throne against such an eventuality.

2. After Constantinople fell to the Turks in 1453, Zoe (her name was changed to Sophia upon her baptism into the Russian Orthodox Church) fled to Rome. There the Pope offered her his protection, hoping to return her to power in Constantinople some day, thereby bringing Asia Minor under the sway of the Latin Church.

3. Bessarion, who had been Metropolitan of Nicaea before the Florentine Union, had championed the reunion of the eastern and western Churches. After the Council of Ferrara-Florence he was appointed a cardinal of the Latin Church. Bessarion was instrumental in arranging the negotiations that led to the marriage of Zoe Paleologos and Ivan III.

4. Nicholas Poppel had represented the Holy Roman Emperor on diplomatic missions to Spain, England and other parts of Europe. He was sent to Moscow by the Emperor as his agent for determining the power and position of the Russian grand prince. The Emperor apparently intended that Poppel establish with the Russians an alliance against the Turks.

5. The Holy Roman Emperor, Maximilian, deluded Ivan III with the hope that he would marry the grand prince's daughter. Maximilian hoped this stratagem would secure Ivan's help for the Emperor's recovery of Hungary.

6. Mengli-Girey's greatest service to the Prince of Moscow was rendered in 1480, during Ivan's famous confrontation with Khan Ahmad on the Ugra River. The Crimean Khan launched an attack into Lithuania that prevented Polish and Lithuanian armies from moving against Ivan while he attempted to lift the Mongol yoke.

CHAPTER III   MUSCOVY AND THE SOUTH SLAVS

1.   John (Ivan) Alexander was Tsar of Bulgaria from 1331 to 1371. His sister, Helen, married Stefan Dušan of Serbia, creating amicable political relations between the Bulgars and Serbs that allowed them to pursue jointly the dream of conquering Constantinople. But internal discord under Alexander's successor, John (Ivan) Šišman (1371-1393), destroyed Bulgarian unity and weakened the Bulgars, preparing them for further defeats by the Turks.

2.   Stefan Dušan was King and Tsar of Serbia from 1331 to 1355. His reign is remembered as the most brilliant period of Serbian history. While Byzantium was preoccupied with domestic disorders, he conquered Albania, Macedonia, Epirus and Thessaly. Dušan believed that the Byzantines, ravaged by civil war and faced with the growing Turkish menace, would welcome him as a protector and help him gain control of Constantinople. While preparing an attack on the Byzantine capital in 1355, however, Dušan died suddenly at the age of 48.

3.   Constantine Manasses was the author of a world chronicle in verse that recounts events from Biblical times to the accession of Alexius I Comnenus of Byzantium. Manasses' chronicle was popular among the Russians and served as a model for early Russian historical writings.

4.   The text refers to John (Ivan) Asen II (1218-1241), who also aspired to rule Constantinople after the city had been captured by the Fourth Crusade. The Bulgarian Patriarchate was established during Asen's reign, which saw Bulgaria gain a prominence in eastern Christian affairs unparalleled in its history.

5.   Here Miliukov refers to the metropolitans Peter and Alexis, whom we have identified above and who strove to secure amity and political peace and cooperation among the Russian princes.

6.   Euthymius, who became Patriarch of Bulgaria in 1375, had great influence upon later writers in Bulgaria, Serbia and Russia. His biographical accounts of Bulgarian saints and letters to Church dignitaries are important historical sources for the study of the fourteenth century.

7. Although Russians originally used the term "Ishmaelites" to designate the Tatars, the word eventually was applied to all who practiced the Mohammedan faith.

8. Miliukov's quotation here is taken from the account of the capture of Constantinople written by Nestor-Iskander, an unknown author who may have been a Slav captured by the Turks. The author concludes his work with prophetical citations from Methodius and Leo (see below), in which this famous misquotation occurs. The word *rusyi* means "blond;" hence, the "prophets" were predicting a reconquest of Constantinople by a blond, Christian people.

9. Methodius of Olympos (Methodius of Patara) was a Greek Father of the third century whose semi-apocryphal writings on the anti-Christ and other themes were translated into Slavic. Leo VI, the Wise, was Emperor of Byzantium from 886 to 912. Leo was renowned for his wisdom largely because of his codification of imperial law (the *Basilica*), which comprised the greatest legal collection in Byzantine history. The author of over one hundred legislative novels, Leo also composed sermons, hymns and other religious works, which include the "prophetic" elements under discussion here.

10. St. Sophia, the great basilica of Constantinople, was revered throughout the eastern Christian world as the mother church of Orthodoxy. By extension, it symbolized the ecclesiastical supremacy of the Byzantine Church over the Slavic peoples.

CHAPTER IV   MOSCOW, THE THIRD ROME

1. Russians of the fifteenth century were convinced that God had created the world in 5508 B. C. Because Scripture states that "a thousand years are as a single day for God," and because the year 1492 would be the 7,000th since creation, the cosmic week would therefore come to an end in 1492, with the final judgment following.

2. The *Paskhaliia* were calendars by which the seasons of Easter were calculated by the Russian Church. Inasmuch as the end of the world was expected in 1492, the liturgical seasons of the Church were compiled only to that date. When the last judgment failed to materialize, Metropolitan Zosima, a figure prominent in the history of the heresy of the Judaizers in Russia, extended the liturgical cycle for another millenium.

3. Filofei (Philotheus) has won renown as the writer who coined the phrase, "Moscow, the Third Rome." For an honest appraisal of his originality, ingenuity and literary worth, see Dmitrij Čiževskij, *History of Russian Literature from the Eleventh Century to the End of the Baroque* ('s-Gravenhage, 1971), pp. 275-279.

4. Mikhail Grigorievich Misiur-Munekhin was the appointed local administrator (*namestnik*) of Pskov from 1510 to 1528. In addition to his introduction of the "Chronograph," he is remembered as a correspondent of the monk Filofei.

5. Vladimir Monomakh, who was grand prince of Rus from 1113 to 1125, was born of a Greek princess who had married Prince Vsevolod I, probably in 1052.

6. The Nemanja dynasty, founded by Stephen Nemanja (1168-1196), ruled the Serbs for two centuries until the Ottoman conquest. During the early years of this dynasty Bulgarian influence over the Serbs was ended and the Serbian Church became autocephalous.

7. The "Tale" begins with an account of the Biblical flood, then lists the important rulers of antiquity, beginning with the ancient Egyptians. The Russian Rurikid family is introduced as part of the family of Caesar Augustus, as Miliukov indicates.

8. Constantine IX Monomachus (ruled 1042-1055) was Byzantine Emperor at the time of the "Cerularian schism" that estranged the eastern and western Churches. His foreign policy, which was highly ineffective, was troubled not only by Persian aggression but by raids on imperial territory mounted by Russia's neighbors and rivals, the Patzinaks.

**CHAPTER V   HERESY, MYSTICISM AND
                                COUNTER IDEOLOGY**

1. The Bogomil Heresy (or Bogomilism) was initiated in the tenth century by a Bulgarian priest, Bogomilu. Adherents of this movement rejected much of the Old Testament, reviled the established Church and maintained a dualistic theology that agreed in many particulars with the teachings of the medieval western sect of the Cathari. Bogomilism also possessed important social significance, in that it reacted against the domination of society by the aristocracy and the clergy.

2.   Solun is the ancient name for the city of Thessalonica.

3.   The heresy of the Judaizers originated in Novgorod and Pskov during the closing decades of the fifteenth century, then spread to Moscow, where it won many converts, including the daughter-in-law of Ivan III. That the heretics also espoused the secularization of ecclesiastical lands and monastic wealth was a point that won them the tolerance of the grand prince. Early in the sixteenth century the heresy was condemned and its leaders burned at the stake.

4.   Karaites were members of a sect founded in Persia in the eighth century who rejected the Talmud and rabbinical tradition and who regarded the Bible the sole source of Jewish law and practice.

5.   The Orthodox Monastery of Mt. Athos was located on the easternmost of the three prongs of the Chalcide Peninsula. Known for its rigid asceticism, Mt. Athos was also an important intellectual center of the eastern Christian world.

6.   Gregory Sinaites (St. Gregory of Sinai) is credited with popularizing mysticism to the point that the extremism of the Hesychast movement became inevitable. St. Gregory Palamas was responsible for disseminating the ideas of the movement and eventually making Hesychasm acceptable enough to warrant inclusion in Orthodox theology.

7.   The adherent of Hesychasm would sit in solitude, his chin upon his chest and his eyes fixed upon his navel. He then repeated the so-called "Jesus Prayer" ("Lord Jesus Christ, Son of God, have mercy on me") while holding his breath. The practiced adherent could often attain a state of religious ecstasy, in which he saw the "Divine Light," or "Light of Mt. Tabor," supposedly the same light that had appeared to Christ's disciples on Mt. Tabor.

8.   Nil Sorsky also won the temporary favor of the grand prince for urging the secularization of Church lands. His followers practiced rigid asceticism and concentrated on good works and spirituality, ignoring the worldly concerns that occupied many other churchmen. In keeping with Nil's idea that Christianity should never be imposed by force, the "non-possessors" (as they were known to distinguish them from the followers of Joseph of Volokolamsk) were tolerant of unorthodox religious belief and more open to the adoption of foreign ideas and techniques of devotion.

9. Nil's monastery was known officially as the Monastery of St. Cyril Therapont. Located near Beloozero, it was also renowned for its extensive library and the erudition of its brethren.

10. The Russian word used here (*pustynnik*) means "desert dweller." I have chosen to render it simply as "hermit."

11. Gennadius was archbishop of Novgorod during the heresy. Together with Joseph of Volokolamsk, he attempted to convince Muscovite secular authorities that the heretics should be condemned and executed. Indeed, Gennadius even secured for Ivan III's edification and emulation an account of the activities of the Spanish Inquisition.

12. Metropolitan Zosima may have been a heretic himself. In any event, he forcefully opposed those who urged brutal persecution of the heretics. For this he earned the hatred of Joseph of Volokolamsk who, in a letter to the bishop of Suzdal, referred to Zosima as "a foul, evil wolf clothed in pastoral garments."

13. Vasily refers to the intermittent warfare with Lithuania that accompanied his reign.

CHAPTER VI   BOYAR OPPOSITION

1. The Pani were the high aristocracy of the Lithuanian-Polish state. Rich, privileged and often autonomous, the Pani held vast estates and at times maintained personal armies, which they commanded in wartime.

2. A voevoda (the term was borrowed from the Lithuanians) in Muscovy was a military governor or head of a town, who was usually high born. The word also meant a general.

3. The Muscovite council of prominent service noblemen. The *duma* assisted the Tsar in legislation, administration and matters of foreign affairs.

4. Prince Andrei Mikhailovich Kurbsky (1528-1583) was a prominent boyar who probably belonged to the "chosen council" that advised Ivan IV during his early years. While commanding Russian military forces against Livonia, Kurbsky deserted his army and sought refuge in Lithuania, whence he is said to have composed his famous letters to Ivan the Terrible in which he castigates his cruelty and defends the Russian nobility against the Tsar's autocratic power. His *History of the Great Prince of Moscow* also attacks Ivan for his persecution of princes and boyars, his savagery toward the Russian people and his abuse of political power. On the controversy concerning the authenticity of Kurbsky's writings, see Edward L. Keenan, *The Kurbskii-Groznyi Apocrypha* (Cambridge, Mass., 1971).

5. That is, his capital city. On how Russians understood the word "yurt" when it was applied to the Muslim world, see J. L. I. Fennell, *Prince A. M. Kurbsky's History of Ivan IV* (Cambridge, 1965), pp. 64n, 89n.

6. Ivan Yurievich Shigona Podzhogin became perhaps Tsar Vasily's closest adviser, often representing the Tsar at important functions and negotiations (such as the negotiations that preceded Russia's recovery of the city of Smolensk). Despite the low status of his family, Shigona Podzhogin was also able to secure for his brother the position of Russian ambassador to the Khanate of Kazan.

7. Ivan refers to the five provinces (*piatiny*) that formed the original territory of the principality of Novgorod.

8. The chosen council (*izbrannaia rada*) is the term by which historians designate the circle of advisers to Ivan IV between 1547 and 1560. These collaborators urged Ivan to undertake the series of reforms that cause this period of Ivan's reign to be regarded the "good years" of his rule.

9. Alexis Adashev was of humble origin, descended from a family that had been servitors of the grand princes of Moscow but had failed to acquire aristocratic rank. When Ivan finally emancipated himself from the control and influence of the chosen council, Adashev was arrested on Ivan's command and died in prison at Dorpat in 1561, perhaps by his own hand.

10. Vassian Patrikeev was the son of Prince Ivan Patrikeev, who had opposed Ivan III by supporting intrigues against his centralizing policies and denouncing his foreign policy against Lithuania. Prince Ivan Patrikeev was ultimately arrested and forced to become a monk. The entire Patrikeev clan earlier had made many enemies in court circles by supporting (and probably adhering to) the non-possessing movement of Nil Sorsky and his followers.

11. The "prince of North Russia" was Prince Vasily Shemiakin of Novgorod-in-Severia, who was accused of maintaining secret relations with King Sigismund of Lithuania. When the metropolitan, Daniel, promised him safe passage, Vasily came to Moscow to answer the charges against him. Vasily died in prison six years after his arrest.

12. Maxim the Greek, a monk of Mt. Athos, had studied in Greece and Italy, where he became a disciple of Savonarola. Invited to Russia in 1515 by Vasily III, Maxim engaged in translation and literary work for the Russian Church. But Maxim expressed many notions that earned him the distrust of Russian civil and ecclesiastical authorities. He proposed the subordination of the Russian Church to the Patriarchate of Constantinople, urged the Muscovite government to liberate Balkan Christians through a war against the Turks, denounced social evils, ignorance and obscurantism in Russia and supported the Trans-Volga Hermits. He was condemned for corrupting holy texts through his translations and was confined in monasteries in Volokolamsk and Tver.

13. That is, he was a follower of Sorsky's Trans-Volga Hermits.

14. Ivan Semenovich Peresvetov (Ivashka was his familiar nickname) addressed two petitions to Ivan IV and composed several political pamphlets in which he lamented the oppressions of the boyars and supported the idea of absolute monarchy.

15. The author of this piece is unknown still.

16. "Feeding" (*kormlenie*) was the system of local administration whereby the grand prince's local agents were entitled, in lieu of salary, to secure their maintenance and provisions from the local populace.

17. The Place of the Brow (*Lobnoe mesto*) was an elevated structure near the Kremlin wall in Moscow from which the Tsar and other officials addressed the populace or read proclamations.

18. This concludes the indirect response to Peresvetov, who offered other measures for the eradication of "injustice," as we shall see below. (Miliukov's note)

19. Fearing civil strife following his death, Vasily III upon his death bed created a regency of advisers to govern the state under the supervision of his widow, Elena. During the early years of Ivan IV's life, members of this regency and their rivals caused great chaos and intrigue in the highest circles of government.

20.   Sylvester, a priest of Novgorod, was apparently summoned to Moscow by Metropolitan Macarius in 1542. In later years he became a very important member of the chosen council. Ivan IV accused him sharply of usurping the royal power and reducing Ivan himself to a mere figurehead.

21.   Artemy was a monk from Pskov who greatly admired the teachings and aspirations of Maxim the Greek. Although he was probably orthodox in his religious views, Artemy was condemned for heresy by a Church council in 1554-1555. He later fled Russia and resided in Lithuania until his death around 1574.

22.   That is, the Solovki Monastery, which had been founded on the Solovki Islands in the White Sea.

23.   Metropolitan Macarius (1542-1563) had been archbishop of Novgorod, where he had won great renown for his scholarship, piety and charity toward his people. A strict follower of the teachings of Joseph of Volokolamsk, Macarius had great influence upon Ivan IV while the metropolitan was a leading member of the chosen council. Macarius is also credited with tempering the explosive passions of the young Tsar and inspiring him to launch the reforms that distinguish Ivan's "good years" of rule.

24.   This council was later termed the *Stoglav* ("Hundred Chapters") because its final pronouncements were issued in a document of one hundred articles.

25.   *Zemskie sobory* (singular, *zemskii sobor*), or assemblies of the land, were councils originally convoked by Ivan IV in 1549 and 1566. In Ivan's day membership in the *sobory* apparently was limited to prominent boyars, important military servitors and certain administrators. During the Time of Troubles, however, the *sobory* gained more representative membership and often functioned as the supreme authority of the land. In the reigns of Michael (1613-1645) and Alexis (1645-1676) the *sobory* met frequently to advise the sovereign on crucial matters of domestic and foreign policy. During the second half of the seventeenth century the *sobory* were bypassed quietly as the Romanovs centralized state power in their own hands.

CHAPTER VII   ROOTS OF POPULAR OPPOSITION

1.   Peresvetov refers to the system of *mestnichestvo*, or hierarchy of ranks, according to which Muscovite princes and boyars were ranked by a complicated genealogical succession. The Tsar was expected to follow this ranking when choosing individuals for key positions in his army and administration. The system persisted until 1682, when the registers of rank were burned at the command of Tsar Feodor.

2.   The *oprichnina* was the bizarre creation of Ivan IV to wreak vengeance upon his real or imagined enemies. Dividing his realm into two parallel administrations, the *oprichnina* and the *zemshchina*, Ivan gave the former to his new favorites, the *oprichniki*, for their control and administration. In this sector the estates of many boyars and princes were seized by the *oprichniki*, who murdered or resettled their former owners. For an assessment of the *oprichnina*, see S. F. Platonov, *Ivan the Terrible*, ed. and trans. by Joseph L. Wieczynski (Gulf Breeze, Florida: Academic International Press, 1974).

3.   The Cheremis were a tribe of Finno-Ugrian origin who lived in the lower basin of the Oka River.

CHAPTER VIII   THE TRIUMPH OF THE NATIONALISTIC PROGRAM

1.   For illustrations of the royal regalia and the Tsarist throne with hip roof and shutters, see Arthur Voyce, *The Art and Architecture of Medieval Russia* (Norman, 1967), plates 163, 164, 180, 181.

2.   Stefan Bathory, a Hungarian, was elected King of Poland in 1575. Bathory believed that coexistence between Poland and Russia was impossible and convinced Polish magnates that war should be carried against Ivan the Terrible. By 1582 Bathory had recovered from Ivan all the Tsar's earlier acquisitions in Livonia and had invaded Russian territory, laying seige to Pskov.

3.   Bathory was descended from a family distinguished only for its service to the Emperor. Prior to his election to the Polish throne, Bathory had served as governor of Transylvania, where his able

administration had won him renown. Among those who particularly respected Bathory's abilities was the Turkish Sultan, who placed Bathory's name in nomination for the crown of Poland.

4. In the early Christian world the term "Patriarch" had been used only to designate the prelates of the four principal sees of Christendom: Alexandria, Antioch, Jerusalem and Rome. A Christian bishop could secure this title only by demonstrating that his municipal church had been founded originally by one of Christ's twelve apostles and that his city had been one of the leading metropolitan centers of the Roman Empire. Constantinople was later granted a Patriarchate in violation of the first term of this condition. Moscow obviously satisfied neither requirement. Hence, the Orthodox Church listed Moscow last in the formal ranking of the Patriarchates.

5. The Tsar's *barmy*, translated earlier as "mantles," were collars or mantles of black silk studded with various jewels and gold. They were considered part of the royal insignia, or regalia.

6. Since Babylonian times, if not earlier, purple had been regarded the color of imperial royalty. The Byzantine emperors spoke of their imperial family as those who had been "born into the purple" (Porphyrogenitus).

7. Here Miliukov refers to the events of January 5, 1565. Having suddenly abdicated and retired to Aleksandrovsk, Ivan informed the people of Moscow that he would no longer rule as Tsar unless he were permitted to deal with traitors summarily and to destroy the "treason" that he imagined on all sides. A crowd of Muscovite petitioners, led by the archbishop of Novgorod and the archimandrite of the Chudov Monastery, then visited Ivan at his retreat and urged him to resume his reign, granting his conditions. For an exposition and analysis of this event, see Sergei Platonov, *Ivan the Terrible*, ed. and trans. by Joseph L. Wieczynski (Gulf Breeze, Florida: Academic International Press, 1974).

CHAPTER IX   SOCIAL CLASSES AND TSARIST AUTOCRACY

1. Ivan Bolotnikov, a former Turkish galley slave, incited social rebellion against the government of Tsar Vasily Shuisky. With an army of serfs, slaves and other social malcontents from the southern Russian lands Bolotnikov marched on Moscow in 1606. In their path Bolotnikov's followers murdered landlords, seized land and property and proclaimed social warfare. After his defeat by loyal forces in 1607, Bolotnikov was captured and put to death.

2. Kuz'ma Minin, a butcher of Nizhni Novgorod, raised the finances needed to equip an army to liberate Moscow from Polish occupation during the closing stages of the Time of Troubles. In September, 1612 this army, with Minin serving as its treasurer, stormed the Polish garrison in Moscow and drove the Poles from the Kremlin, thereby ending foreign intervention in Russian national affairs.

3. After the deposition of Tsar Vasily Shuisky in 1610, the Muscovites decided to offer the crown to Wladyslaw, the son of King Sigismund III of Poland (who will be identified more fully below). But it readily became apparent upon Wladyslaw's accession that Sigismund intended to create in Moscow a source of personal support to champion his own aspirations to rule the Russian state. Sigismund introduced to the Russian capital many individuals whom Russians often termed "the very worst people:" peasants, scribes and minor servitors. In so doing the Polish King sought allegiance from native, low-born Russians who would value his patronage. Among these "very worst people" was Feodor (Fedka) Andronov, whom Muscovites regarded a "trading peasant" because of his humble origins. Andronov and other commoners were then allowed to participate in the business of government, much to the alarm and disgust of the higher strata of Muscovite society.

4. During the summer of 1610 two armies stood before Moscow. One, commanded by the second False Dmitry, championed radical social causes and attracted the support of Russian lower classes. The second, led by King Sigismund of Poland, represented social attitudes that were more conservative and therefore more acceptable to the Muscovite boyars. The boyars and other influential conservatives resolved to terminate the Time of Troubles by offering the Russian throne to Prince

Wladyslaw, Sigismund's son. Wladyslaw was then named Tsar under a set of conditions designed to preserve Russian political and religious independence and the influence of the boyars in matters of foreign policy.

5.　The *deti boiarskie* (singular, *syn boiarskii*) were lesser Muscovite gentry who comprised the largest segment of the military servitors of the Russian state.

6.　An *uezd*, or district, was a county in which were concentrated the administrative and judicial responsibilities for a town and its rural dependencies.

7.　In Muscovite times *tarkhan* charters were deeds bestowing exemption from taxation or other immunities upon privileged individuals. Such charters also removed an individual from intermediate state authority and subordinated him directly to the Tsar or Grand Prince.

8.　When the second False Dmitry advanced with an army against Moscow, his forces established their headquarters at the village of Tushino, several miles northwest of Moscow.

9.　When Vasily Shuisky failed to dislodge the forces of the second False Dmitry from Tushino, he sent Michael Vasilievich Skopin-Shuisky, his relative, to Novgorod to raise an army of loyal subjects and to recruit foreign mercenaries, especially Swedes. Skopin then moved southward with his army, drawing to his banner loyalists from Kostroma, Yaroslavl and other northern towns, until his forces were sufficiently powerful to attack Tushino. Early in 1610 the second False Dmitry, apprehensive of Skopin's growing might, abandoned Tushino and fled to Kaluga, southwest of Moscow.

10.　"Muzhik" was a term Muscovites often used to designate those of humble origin. Frequently it was applied to the peasant as a term of derision.

11.　*Gosti* (singular, *gost'*) were the richest members of the Russian merchant class, who held this title as an honorary award from the Tsar. They were expected to serve the government by collecting taxes, regulating government trade and performing other duties for central authorities. At certain times they may have numbered as few as thirty men.

12.　After Kuz'ma Minin and others had roused the people of the region of Nizhni Novgorod to march against the Polish occupation of Moscow, Prince Dmitry Mikhailovich Pozharsky was named commander of the national militia sent to free the capital. Pozharsky, barely recovered from wounds received fighting the Poles in 1611, established headquarters in Yaroslavl, then attacked Moscow in October, 1612, routing the Polish garrison.

13. That is, the auxiliary forces that Minin and Pozharsky had mobilized from towns that supported the campaign to drive the Poles from Moscow.

14. The Russian Church, and particularly its Patriarch, Hermogen, urged Russian towns to rebel against the Polish government in Moscow. One of the first to heed this call was the voevoda of Riazan, Prokopy Petrovich Liapunov. Liapunov then contacted the ataman of Tula, Ivan Zarutsky, and the prominent Prince of Kaluga, Dmitry Trubetskoi. This triumvirate agreed to mount operations against the Poles from Serpukhov and Kolomna. When dissension in their ranks threatened to abort their efforts, the three allies signed the pact to which Miliukov refers here, pledging themselves to restrict their own powers and to pursue social and agrarian objectives acceptable to "the entire land." For particulars, see S. F. Platonov, *The Time of Troubles*, translated by John T. Alexander (Lawrence, 1970), pp. 134-141.

15. Hetman Stanislaw Ziolkowski was perhaps the most able military commander and most far-seeing statesman among the Polish forces that invaded Russia during the Time of Troubles. Although he had arranged the negotiations that led to the acceptance of Wladyslaw as Tsar of Russia, Ziolkowski warned King Sigismund that Russians would react violently against the Polish presence in Moscow, if the limitations imposed upon Wladyslaw were not observed. When Sigismund flaunted his advice, Ziolkowski returned to Poland, relinquishing his military command to Gosiewski.

CHAPTER X   SERVICE PEOPLE, AUTOCRACY AND THE TIME OF TROUBLES

1. The *sudebnik* was a codification of Russian law. Issued by Ivan III in 1497 and reformed by Ivan IV in 1550, this code was the principal legal manual of the Russian state.

2.   It was customary in Muscovy to refer the guilt of an individual to
his entire family. A whole clan could be subject to exile, confiscations
and other reprisals because of the derelictions of any one of its members.

3.   Following Ziolkowski's return to Poland, King Sigismund allowed
Alexander Gosiewski to form a military dictatorship that completely disregarded the conditions imposed earlier upon Prince Wladyslaw. Russian boyars, who had originally supported the notion of Polish rule in
Russia to preserve their own interests, were humiliated and barred from
any effective role in this new regime. When it became apparent that
Gosiewski's dictatorial manner was merely prelude to Sigismund's assumption of personal control of Russian affairs, Russian patriots were stirred
to adopt the course of action that quickly resulted in the expulsion of the
Poles from Moscow.

4.   During the seventeenth century the term *zemskii sovet* was synonymous with the national assembly (*zemskii sobor*) discussed above.

5.   The formal act of election, which had to be accompanied by a
written deed, or "agreement," is indicated by the solemn title used by
Pozharsky: "Through election by all ranks of people in the Russian
state, the *stolnik* and voevoda of military and civil affairs, Dmitry Pozharsky and his comrades." This was a literal repetition of the intro-
ductory portions of the agreement with Trubetskoi. (Miliukov's note)

6.   When the Cossacks encamped before Moscow realized that Liapunov
would countenance legislation certain to hasten the process of enserf-
ment, they lured Liapunov to a meeting and murdered him in July, 1611.

**CHAPTER XI   THE ASSEMBLY OF THE LAND AND THE
                 CRISIS OF AUTOCRACY**

1.   Peter Vockerodt was secretary of the Prussian embassy in Russia
during the closing years of the reign of Peter the Great. A keen observer
and an ardent compiler of data, Vockerodt's reminiscences are an especially reliable and valuable source for the study of Petrine Russia. That
Vockerodt was one of the few foreigners serving in Russia who was
fluent in Russian adds to his credibility.

2.   Grigory Karpovich Kotoshikhin was a clerk in the Russian Foreign
Office who betrayed Russian diplomatic secrets to Sweden, then fled to

that country in 1664. He changed his surname to Selitsky, renounced
Orthodoxy for Protestantism and served the Swedish government as
an authority on Russian affairs. His book, *On Russia in the Reign of
Alexis Mikhailovich,* is a valuable, albeit biased, account of the institutions, beliefs, habits and foibles of Muscovites in the seventeenth century.

3.   Filaret Romanov, an early rival of Boris Godunov for the Russian
throne, had been arrested by the Poles after the collapse of the Polish
venture in Moscow in 1612. His release from imprisonment was one of
the provisions of the Treaty of Deulino, signed by the Russians and Poles
in 1618. For a masterly account of the career of Godunov and developments between the death of Ivan the Terrible and the onset of the Time
of Troubles, see S. F. Platonov, *Boris Godunov: Tsar of Russia*, ed. and
trans. by L. Rex Pyles (Gulf Breeze, Florida: Academic International
Press, 1973).

4.   Filaret's war with Poland (1632-1634) erupted when a ten-year truce,
stipulated by the Treaty of Deulino, expired. The war ended without
significant gain by either side. Poland received an indemnity but was obliged to withdraw all claims to the Russian throne enjoyed by Wladyslaw.

CHAPTER XII   THE RISE OF THE BUREAUCRACY

1.   The Nogais, or Nogai Tatars, controlled the northern shores of the
Caspian Sea, the basin of the Yaik River and the region east of the Lower
Volga River.

2.   The *chernye slobody* were settlements of merchants and artisans
directly subordinate to state administration, rendering services directly
to the state. Most were located in the suburbs of important towns.

3.   "Sworn men" (*tseloval'niki*) were officials elected by peasant communities or towns to discharge administrative, financial and judicial
services for the state. Sworn men also attended local courts, ensuring
that justice was being served by local judges. They took their oath
of office by kissing the cross or the Bible, from which practice their
Russian title (literally, "cross kissers") derives.

4.   "Lower police servitors" (*iaryzhnye*) were individuals recruited
from tax-paying communities to serve primarily as messengers, watch-
men and in similar, rather menial capacities.

**CHAPTER XIII   IMPACT OF THE WEST UPON RUSSIAN
NATIONAL SELF-CONSCIOUSNESS**

1. Boris Godunov sent some eighteen Russian youths abroad for the
study of foreign languages. Three groups of six each were dispatched to
England, France and Lübeck. Miliukov here refers to Nikifor A. Gri-
goriev, who renounced his Orthodox faith and later became a member
of the Episcopalian clergy in England.

CHAPTER XIV   WESTERN INFLUENCES IN EVERYDAY LIFE

1. Ovoshchny Riad (literally, "Vegetable Row") was a street in the
commercial section of Moscow where various goods were sold by Russian and foreign merchants from individual stalls or small shops.

2. Inasmuch as Russians used the term "Germans" to designate both
inhabitants of the German area and foreigners in general, translation of
the word poses special problems. Prior to the reign of Peter I the term
usually denoted foreigners from northern and western Europe.

3. Boris Ivanovich Morozov, a prominent Russian boyar, was a great
admirer of Western customs and learning. As tutor of the Tsar's
children, Morozov used German books and engravings in his teaching
and attempted to instill in his charges an appreciation of European
ways by dressing them in German clothing.

4. The domra was a stringed musical instrument, much like a mandolin,
that often was used to accompany the telling of historical or fabled
narratives.

5. For a spirited discussion of these and similar antics at Michael's court,
see R. N. Bain, *The First Romanovs* (New York, 1967), pp. 26-29.

6. Tsar Alexis ordered the destruction of musical instruments and actors' masks not only in the Moscow region but throughout Russia.
This decree was aimed at curtailing the popularity of the *skomorokhi*,
itinerant musicians, actors and entertainers who had figured promi-
nently in Russian folk culture since Kievan times. The Church regarded
these entertainers as an unwholesome remnant of Russia's pagan past.

7. Artamon Sergeevich Matveev, a close personal friend of Tsar Alexis, was head of the Foreign Office and one of the Tsar's most trusted advisers. Often considered an important precursor of Peter the Great, Matveev was renowned for his enlightenment, scholarship and deep interest in European culture. His home in Moscow contained many western paintings, carpets, clocks and other novelties unknown to Russians. Natalia Kirillevna Naryshkina was educated by Matveev. Matveev and his Scottish wife instilled in the young girl an independence of mind and manner that contrasted with staid Muscovite habits. At the age of seventeen Natalia met Alexis in Matveev's home and married the Tsar early in 1672.

8. The drama apparently was based upon Christopher Marlowe's play, "Tamburlaine the Great."

9. Drama was introduced to German lands by touring English troupes, who emphasized comedy in their repertoire. Most often the clown of such comedies was named "Pickelherring." Miliukov probably refers to this stage name, rather than to a specific playwright.

10. Preobrazhenskoe was the site of the Tsar's wooden country house, set in a forest on the bank of the Yaitsa River, about two miles from the Foreign Settlement.

CHAPTER XV THE FOREIGNER IN SEVENTEENTH-CENTURY RUSSIA

1. Devlet-Girey was Khan of the Crimean Tatars. In 1571 the Khan led an army of at least 40,000 men to Moscow, where he defeated Russian forces, then ravaged and burned much of the city. Moscow's southern suburbs and much of the Kremlin and Kitai-Gorod were consumed by flames. After looting the outskirts of the city, the Khan withdrew with thousands of Russian captives.

2. The *streltsy* were the first permanent infantry units created in the Muscovite armed forces. Ivan the Terrible established units of some 5,000 streltsy in Moscow and positioned an additional 7,000 in other towns. In Moscow the *streltsy* lived in private communities, engaged in business and commerce and were exempt from taxation. During peacetime they served the government as policemen, firemen and in other capacities.

3. Miliukov refers to the Livonian War waged by Ivan IV (1558-1563 and 1578-1582). For an interesting account of the settling of foreign prisoners throughout Russia, see S. F. Platonov's *Moscow and the West,* ed. and trans. by Joseph L. Wieczynski (Hattiesburg, Miss.: Academic International Press, 1972) pp. 14-18. This work also parallels many of the events and attitudes Miliukov treats in this chapter.

**CHAPTER XVI   THE IMPACT OF WESTERN FAITH AND
                  LITERATURE ON RUSSIA**

1. Patrick Gordon (1635-1699) was one of the leading collaborators of Peter the Great. Having served in the Swedish and Polish armies, Gordon joined the Russian service in 1661 and rose to the rank of general. He commanded Russian forces in campaigns against the Crimea and Azov and constantly advised Peter on military affairs. Although he wished to return to the West during his later years, his importance to the Russian government caused his many requests for this permission to be refused.

2. Afanasy Lavrentievich Ordyn-Nashchokin (1605-1681), though of humble origin, won the friendship of Tsar Alexis and boyar rank, then became director of the Russian Foreign Office. He much appreciated the European political and economic systems of the seventeenth century and became a spokesman for mercantilism in Russia. He urged Tsar Alexis to devote his foreign policy to the objective of acquiring territory in the Baltic region, from which western influences could penetrate Russia more easily.

3. Prince Boris Golitsyn was cousin to Vasily Golitsyn, the favorite of Peter the Great's half-sister, Sophia. Extremely interested in western culture (he spoke Latin fluently), Golitsyn first introduced Peter to the Foreign Settlement, an experience that determined the Tsar's early education and much of his subsequent activity.

4. Lazar Baranovich was archbishop of Chernigov. Renowned as a preacher, Baranovich modeled his homilies upon examples of Jesuit oratory then unknown in Great Russia. Baranovich visited Moscow when the Russian court was greatly influenced by the learning of another Ukrainian scholar, Semen Polotsky.

5. The Muscovite Printing Office (*Pechatnyi dvor*) had been founded
by Ivan the Terrible in the middle of the sixteenth century to serve
as the official agency for printing and distributing books approved for
circulation by the Muscovite government.

6. Evfimy, a monk of the Chudov Monastery, was a trusted colleague
of Patriarch Nikon. In 1652 Nikon appointed Evfimy editor of the
Printing Office. Upon Ivan Nasedka's resignation, Evfimy was named
chief editor of the Printing Office by Tsar Alexis. Evfimy then col-
laborated with Nikon in launching the ecclesiastical innovations that occasioned the schism in the Russian Church.

7. In 1682 a Slavic-Greek-Latin Academy was chartered to provide
studies in philosophy, theology, grammar, jurisprudence and other subjects. Finally inaugurated in 1687, the Academy intended to strengthen
Orthodoxy by defending it against heresy, blasphemy and unorthodox
books. One contemporary scholar (Vernadsky) has termed the Academy
the Russian equivalent of the Inquisition and "an attempt to establish
the church's strict control over the education of all Russians and forcibly
to suppress all opposition to such control."

**CHAPTER XVII   NATIONALIST REACTION TO
                   WESTERN INFLUENCE**

1. Paul Déroulède (1846-1914) was a prominent French political figure
who helped to overthrow the Paris Commune in 1871, actively supported
Boulanger and ardently opposed Dreyfus and his supporters. Bitterly
opposed to French republicanism, Déroulède attempted to topple the
French government in 1899 with the help of reactionary military circles.
When this attempted coup ended in failure, Déroulède was exiled in 1900.
He actively supported the proposed Franco-Russian military alliance,
apparently in the hope that French association with Russia would expose
France to more conservative Russian political institutions. His interest
in Tolstoi's teachings is unknown to me.

2. Archbishop Arseny of Thessaly visited Moscow when Metropolitan
Job assumed the position of the first Russian Patriarch. Arseny was
given spiritual charge of a cathedral in Moscow and witnessed the events
of the Time of Troubles, leaving valuable accounts of the period.

3. Marina Mniszech, daughter of a prominent Polish magnate, was betrothed to the first False Dmitry during his sojourn in Poland, then joined him in Moscow after his acceptance by the Russian people.

4. Pastor Martin Baer was the Lutheran minister of the Foreign Settlement. He became notorious among the Russian populace when the first False Dmitry allowed him to conduct religious services in the Muscovite palace for Protestants who attended Dmitry's coronation ceremonies.

5. Here Miliukov probably alludes to experiences he himself underwent in Istanbul after his departure from Russia in 1920 following the collapse of the White armies.

6. Adam Olearius (1599-1671) was a German scholar who visited Russia four times between 1634 and 1643 as envoy from the Duke of Holstein. Inasmuch as he spoke Russian and associated freely with Russians at all levels of society, Olearius' commentaries on the Muscovite state are deemed a major source for the study of Russia during the seventeenth century. An excellent English version of Olearius' writings can be found in Samuel H. Baron, *The Travels of Olearius in Seventeenth-Century Russia* (Stanford, 1967).

7. Deacon Paul of Aleppo, the son of Patriarch Macarius of Antioch, visited Russia on two separate occasions some twenty years after the journeys of Olearius. Inasmuch as he was commissioned to arbitrate the dispute between Tsar Alexis and Patriarch Nikon, he became well acquainted with political and religious affairs in Moscow.

**CHAPTER XVIII   YURY KRIZHANICH AND THE RUSSIAN
                    NATIONALIST TRADITION**

1. In 1667 Moscow was compelled to abandon its claims to Ukrainian territory west of the Dnepr River because the Cossacks of the Ukraine rejected Russian overlordship in favor of union with Poland. The Ukrainian Cossacks also refused to surrender to Russia refugee peasants who had fled their enserfed condition. After 1667 these Cossacks also attempted to enlist the support of the Turks and the Tatars against both Russia and Poland, in order to achieve Ukrainian independence from both countries.

**CHAPTER XXII   KRIZHANICH'S SOCIAL AND
ECONOMIC THEORIES**

1. Major General Ivan Nikitich Boltin (1735-1792) was one of the
most distinguished Russian historians of the eighteenth century.

INDEX